The authors' royalties from the sale of this book are being donated to the Pearl S. Buck Foundation for the benefit of Amerasian children.

THE LAST DAYS

OF

MASH

THE LAST DAYS OF MASH

Photographs and Notes
ARLENE ALDA

Commentary
ALAN ALDA

The Unicorn Publishing House
New Jersey

Published by The Unicorn Publishing House, Inc., 90 Park Avenue, Verona, New Jersey 07044. This book may not be reproduced in whole or in part, by any means, without permission. For information address:

The Unicorn Publishing House, Inc.
90 Park Avenue
Verona, New Jersey 07044
Att: Joseph Scrocco, Jr.

Design: Sharon Brady

Printed in Japan by Dai Nippon Printing Co. Ltd. through DNP (America), Inc.
Special thanks to Mr. Yoh Jinno

EDITORIAL CARTOON SECTION:
Richard Crowson/The Jackson Sun • Tom Meyer/San Francisco Chronicle
Jim Kammerud/Ohio State Lantern • John Backderf/Ohio State Lantern
J.D. Crowe/Copley News Service • Dan DeBellis/The Collegian
Mark Rollins/The Collegian • Wayne Stayskal/Tribune Company Syndicate, Inc.
Robert Krieger/The Province • Paul Rigby/New York Post
Bill Sanders/The Milwaukee Journal • John Trever/Albuquerque Journal
Jim Borgman/King Feature Syndicate • Ray Osrin/The Plain Dealer
Lee Judge/Kansas City Times

Printing History:
1 2 3 4 5 6 7 8 9 10 11 12 13 14 15 16 17 18 19 20
Library of Congress Cataloging in Publication Data

Alda, Arlene, 1933-
   The last days of M*A*S*H.

   1. MASH (Television program) I. Alda, Alan, 1936-   II. Title. III. Title: Last days of MASH.
PN1992.77.M2854A43 1983   791.43'72   83-1803
ISBN 0-88101-009-X
ISBN 0-88101-008-1 (pbk.)

This book is dedicated to Amerasian children;
innocent victims of real war.

Acknowledgements

Countless thanks to the extraordinary cast and crew of MASH, with additional thanks to Martin Bregman, Rosemary Chiaverini, Mary Rapoport, Chuck Panama, Jean Gruder and Joe Scrocco.

Introduction

The MASH set burned to the ground on a Saturday. They called me at about ten o'clock the next morning to let me know. We still had our interiors on the sound stage at 20th Century Fox, but the buildings in the Malibu mountains were destroyed. We were in the middle of filming the two hour movie that would end the MASH series, and there was no way we could shoot the scenes that were left without the exterior sets.

I put the phone down and took my script into the living room to see what changes could be made in the story to accommodate a brush fire. I was amused to realize that what I felt, instead of sadness and loss, was excitement. It was the same feeling I had had as a young actor on the stage when another player would miss an entrance. I would be all alone out there and I would think, with that same little stab of excitement, *"Okay,* let's see what I can make of this." It was the feeling I would have many times years later as we filmed MASH when we would realize that a scene just didn't work and with a calm born of totally irrational confidence, we would put a hand into that thick dark place just beyond our reach and pull out an idea.

Within a few minutes, I realized that some scenes would actually play better against the activity of a bug out as the MASH unit scrambled to escape a brush fire.

An hour later I drove with Burt Metcalfe, the producer of the show, to the mountains near Malibu to see how bad the damage was.

There was nothing left.

Only the "Best Care Anywhere" sign was still standing, and one or two tents.

The big tin hospital building was completely destroyed. It had melted into little puddles on the ground. In every direction, the hills were covered with gray and black ash and were still smoking. We were told by a ranger that the fire had swept through the place at about 40 miles an hour as it made its way down to the sea.

Two days earlier the fire marshall had considered shutting us down because the fire was in a neighboring valley and headed in our direction. It wasn't until I heard how fast the fire had moved that I understood his concern. If we had been there when the fire hit, there would have been no way to move the hundred people in our crew out of the canyon before the fire swept across it. I realized the value of having an objective eye like that of the fire marshall on the set. When you have the right light and the actors are ready, all you want to do is turn the camera. You don't tend to stop just because a fire is headed toward you.

That's the way it was with us.

For eleven years, we didn't stop for anything.

Then we looked up and realized that pretty soon we'd be burned out. And then we stopped.

This is the story of our last few days.

Alan Alda

Publisher's Note

The hand-written notes are by Arlene Alda.
The commentary printed on the bottom of the pages is by Alan Alda.

In October, 1982, a raging brush fire in the Malibu hills destroyed the outdoor MASH set. Ironically, the above sign was one of the few things left relatively untouched. I was stunned to see the devastation.

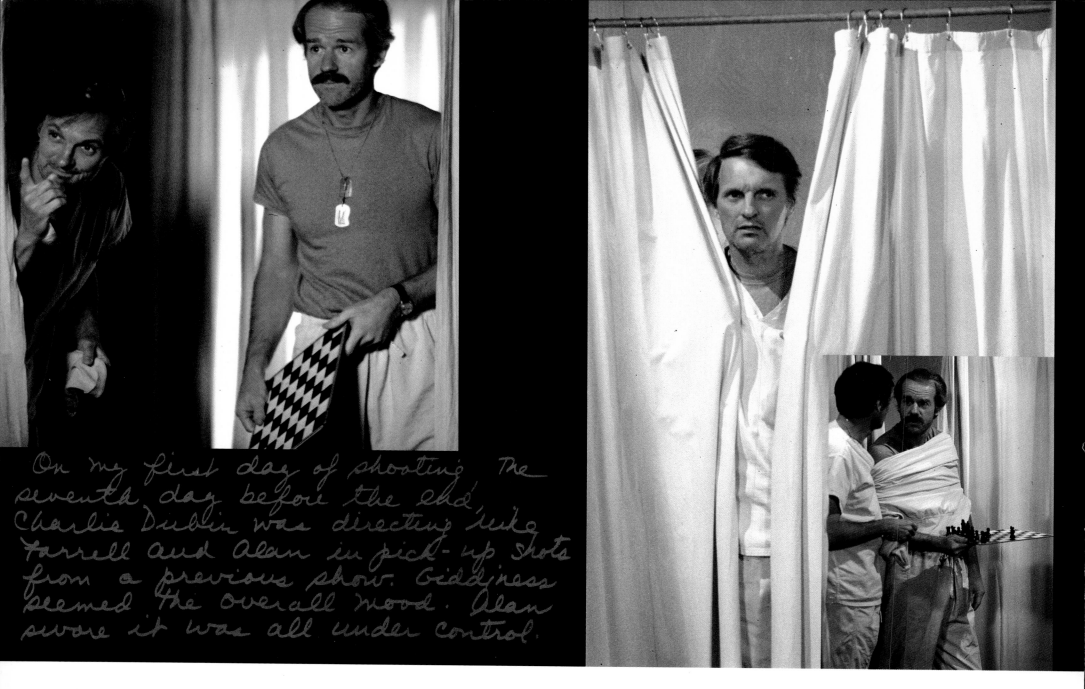

On my first day of shooting The seventh day before the end, Charlie Dublin was directing Mike Farrell and Alan in pick-up shots from a previous show. Giddiness seemed the overall mood. Alan swore it was all under control.

We always worked in a state of controlled nutsiness. Even while kidding and laughing we would be trying to reach that moment where everything clicks—where you say the right words while you pull your shirt off at the right moment, stay in focus, stay in the light, and look life-like.

That same day, David Ogden Stiers and Harry Morgan had to do a scene together. In between takes, both David and Harry broke everyone up with their own hysterical laughter at the number of takes they were doing.

Look in Harry's eye. You'll see a dry but naughty glint. Look at how he makes David Stiers melt. Harry melted us all.

Harry has fallen into David's arms because he has forgotten his lines. It was a rare event for him, but whenever it happened, he always made the most of it.

Harry Morgan was of the opinion that saying lines while getting into a surgical gown was a physical impossibility.

Play is the actor's workplace. We have to step into an imaginary world as if it were real. If we are caught merely *pretending* it is real, the house of cards collapses. But unless an unseen spine of discipline runs through all of this, it will never work.

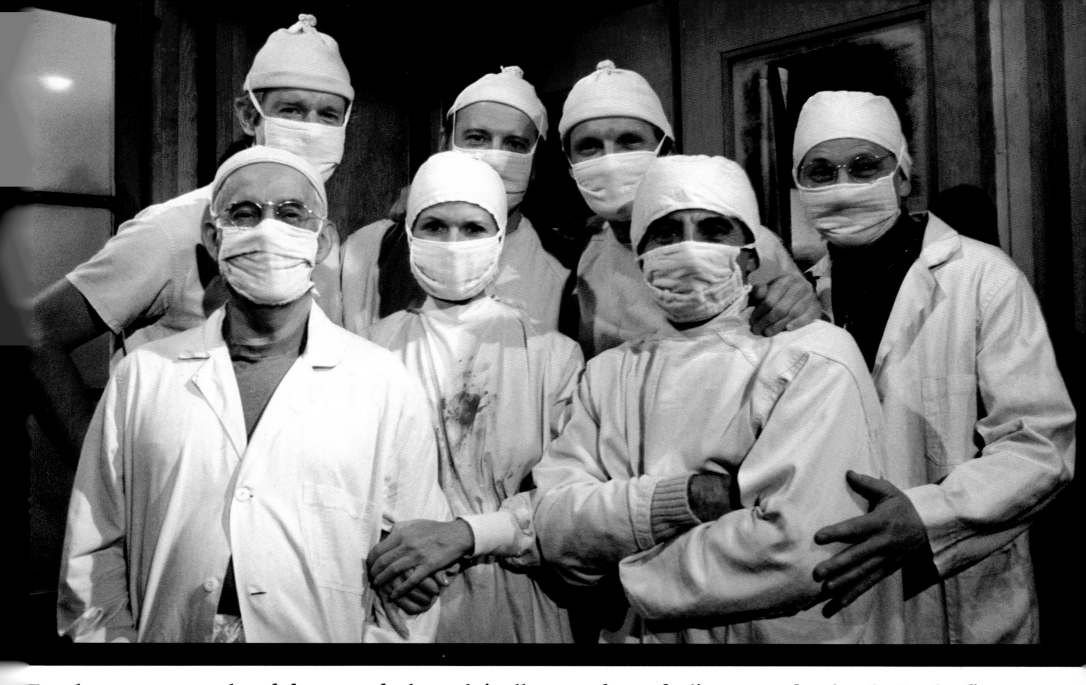

For eleven years we played doctor and, through it all, we took our fooling around seriously. In the first year, I loaned McLean Stevenson a book on the history of medicine. He studied it thoroughly. Months later, when he found someone by the side of the highway who had just been in a car accident, he remembered a passage from the book in such detail that he was able to reach into the open wound and pinch off the carotid artery until help came.

The horsing around, of course, wasn't all noble work in the service of art. We would sneak up behind people and clamp strings of hemostats to their backs and then (lying badly) pretend we hadn't done it. At the end of a shot, we would wad up surgical tape and pelt the sincere thespian who had just been acting his or her heart out.

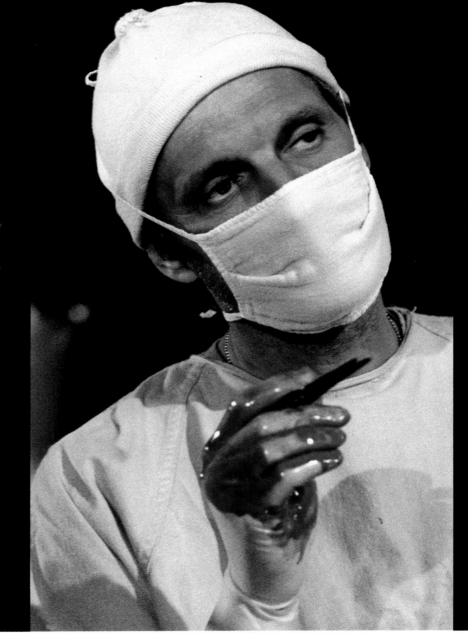

When Alan directs, the blood may be artificial, but the seriousness is real.

The fun tended to come to an abrupt halt for anyone who happened to be directing. Early on in the series the other actors let me know that I had an adequate sense of humor until it came time for me to direct. Then I would say playful things like, "Can we stop the fooling around and have quiet on the set? I'm not going to say this again and I mean it!"

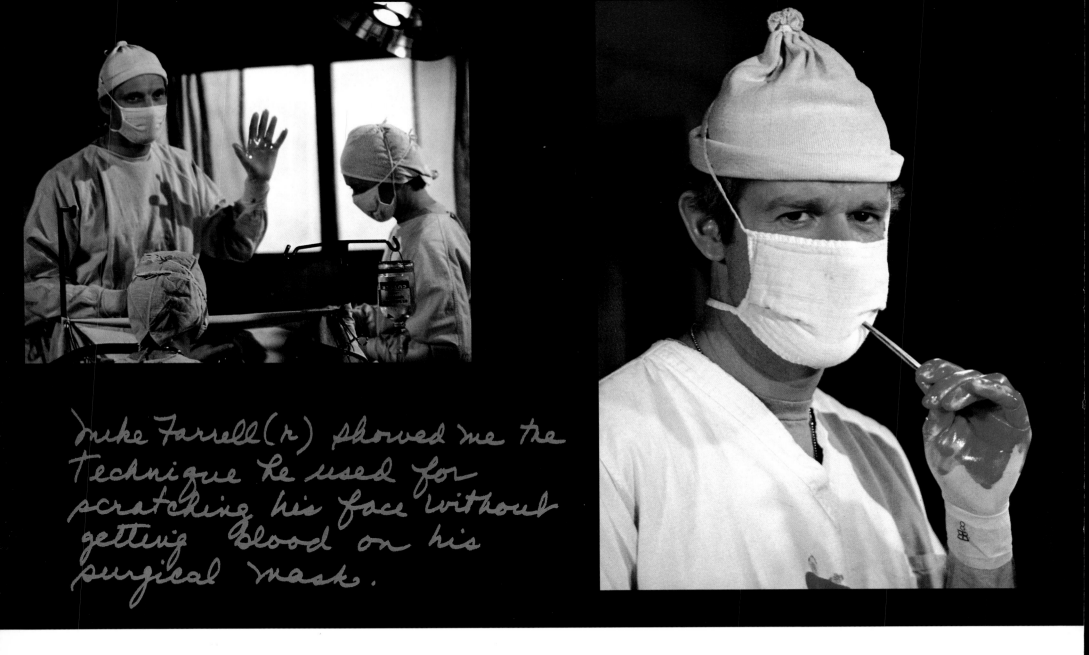

Mike Farrell (r) showed me the technique he used for scratching his face without getting blood on his surgical mask.

In the early years, the blood was okay. It had a nice color, and it ran well. Then the company stopped manufacturing it and the only theatrical blood you could buy was made with a base of caro syrup. It would probably have been all right on waffles, but it stuck to rubber gloves like glue. We tried making our own formulas, even mixing shampoo with red water color, but all that did was turn pink and foam all over us.

Threw a party on the set.

Burt Metcalfe
and Alan

Of the many celebrations that week, it was the only one that was personal and private. Only the cast and crew were invited. Alan usually had Pizza and drinks after shooting on Fridays. This Friday had a more elaborate Italian menu. The main ingredient was unabashed feeling mixed with delicious pasta.

Jan Jorden, Burt's wife typified some of the abandoned joy felt that night.

Burt Metcalfe, who for the last seven years produced the show, became a close friend. We worked so well together that we were able to write for the series at odd hours and peculiar times. One evening, after a full day's shooting, we wrote the entire second act of a show, sitting up late in an Italian restaurant.

I was glad that Loretta Swit and Alan stayed in that dramatic backlighting long enough to get some shots of them.

The cast was together 12 or 14 hours a day, but we seldom had enough time to talk. I would be running from the sound stage to the editing room when Loretta would stop me and start a leisurely conversation. I would shift from foot to foot and finally say something graceful like, "Loretta, you're making me late." After awhile, I noticed her speaking more and more rapidly when we met until, finally, I could hardly understand her at all.

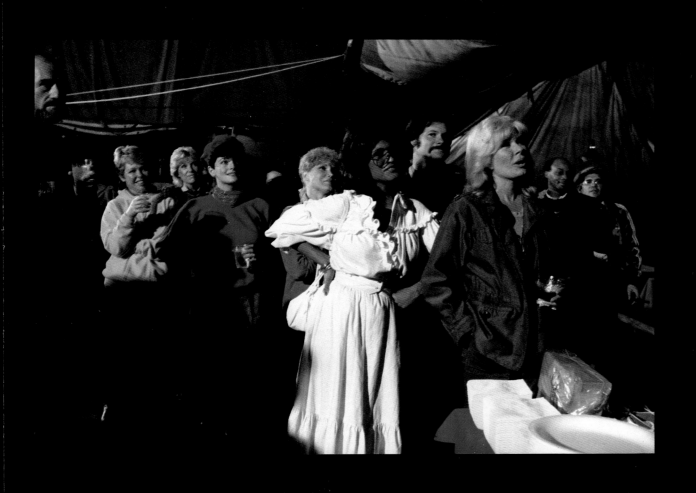

I stood on a chair and thanked everyone for how much they had given—especially the extras. They weren't background, they were actors and it was their show as much as anyone's. We stood looking at one another as we had many times before in scenes like this, only this time we knew we probably wouldn't be seeing each other again.

Marty Lowenheim, dialogue coach, had helped Alan learn his lines for eleven years. According to Alan, he never succeeded. (not Marty's fault.)

We stayed late. No one wanted to leave. People started improvising entertainment.
G.W. Bailey, the gravel voiced Sergeant Rizzo, told a story that he said he always relayed to people who asked him if Alan Alda is really a nice guy. He described me directing the last episode, struggling to get a

difficult shot before the sun hid behind a bank of clouds. Lunch was called and everyone hungrily headed for the food wagon. G.W. Bailey described his surprise as Alda, the Great Humanitarian, sank back in his chair, cursing and pounding his fist saying, ''I'm losing the light, and these bastards have to *eat?*''

The pendulum of mood sometimes swung in tandem...

We were playing the banquet scene from the movie that would end the series and it started to get to us. We would sink into reveries and when laughter would come it would rock us. We couldn't get enough of it.

... except for the moments alone.

We had decided to end the show because we felt it was getting next to impossible to think up new stories and find new ways to stage them and play them.

But as the final day came closer, it became hard to face leaving.

We sat for filmed interviews and answered questions about the show. "Are you like your character?" . . . "Has your character changed over the years?" . . . "Why do you think the show has been so successful?" We had heard all the questions before and the audience had heard the answers. "Yes and No." . . . "Yes and No." . . . and "Search me."

This last photo still makes me yawn.

We got ourselves up for the interviews, but the whole thing had the slightly uncomfortable air of writing our own obituaries. I was that day what I was during the entire 11 years—a little manic, a little thoughtful, a little skeptical and very tired.

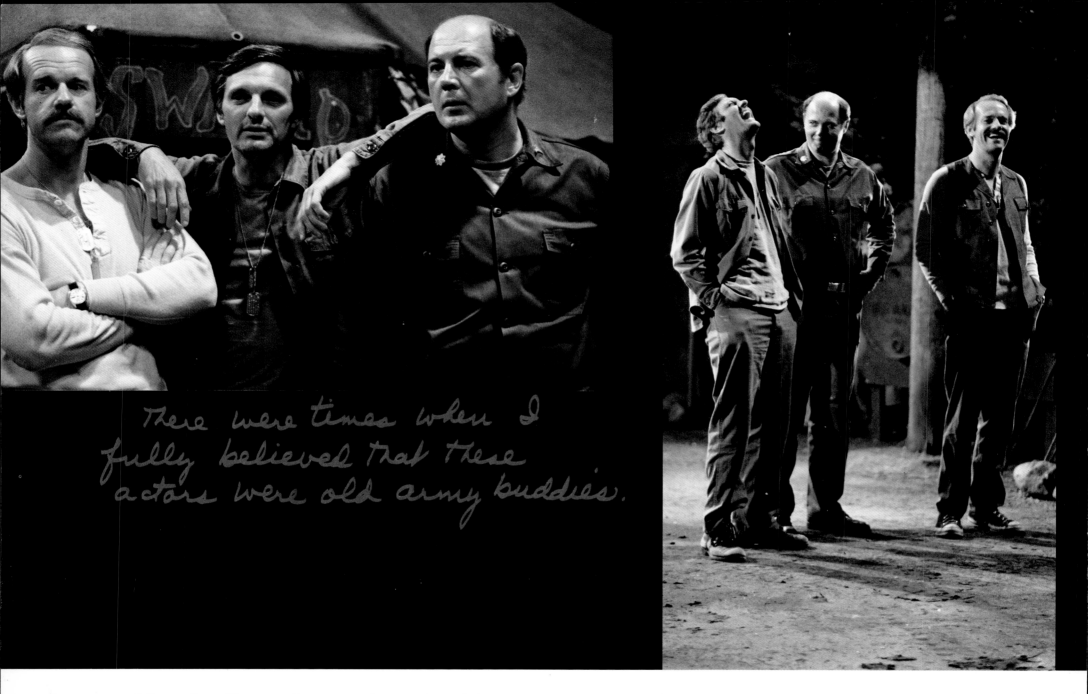

There were times when I fully believed that these actors were old army buddies.

When David and Mike and I stood on the fake rubber dirt floor just outside the swamp, I remembered standing there eight or nine years earlier with Wayne Rogers. I had been acting 12 hours a day in M★A★S★H and co-producing and writing a whole other series at night. The night we taped our first episode, I worked in the control booth until one in the morning, swilling an entire bottle of champagne in celebration.

The next morning, I was totally and completely sick. Fortunately, Wayne and I were playing a hangover scene that morning. We came out of the swamp and I kept walking until I got to the bushes and threw up all over Korea. Not one of my proudest moments. And to paraphrase Laurence Olivier—*acting* a hangover is much easier.

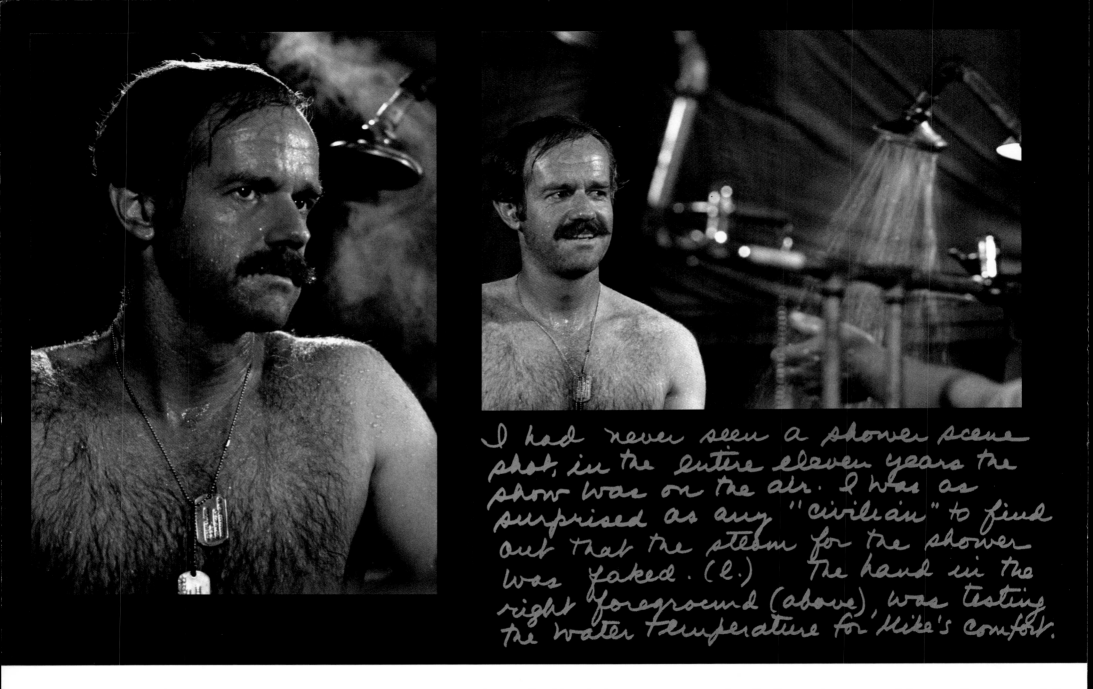

I had never seen a shower scene shot, in the entire eleven years the show was on the air. I was as surprised as any "civilian" to find out that the steam for the shower was faked. (l.) The hand in the right foreground (above), was testing the water temperature for Mike's comfort.

As we worked in the shower that week I remembered all of the scenes we had shot there and how they would often be scheduled at just the wrong time. They would usually come after I had spent a solid week indulging myself in Chinese food. I would often stand there exposed from the waist up wishing I had just a little less Moo Goo Gai Pan hanging from my pectorals.

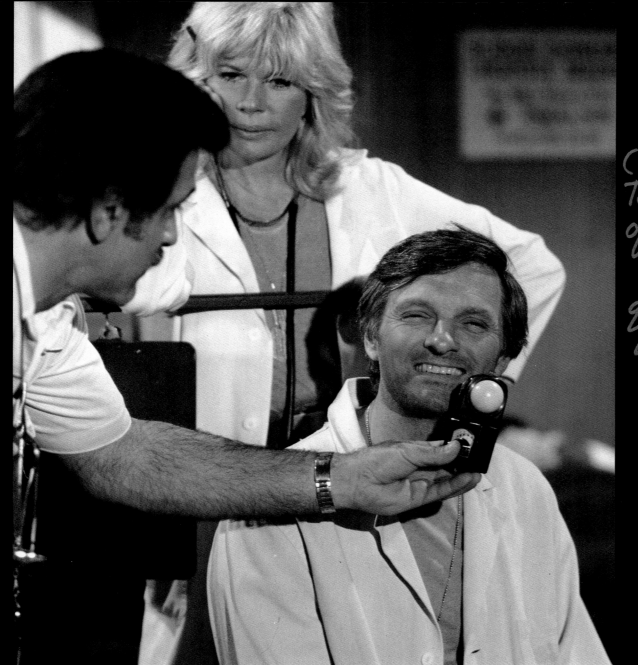

Dominick Palmer
(cinematographer) is
taking a light reading
of Alan's face.
Loretta waits and
quips with Dominick
while he works.

Even when lithe and beautiful, I was a little embarrassed by shower scenes. We were naked except for little flesh-colored bikinis and from the side of the set you could see all our loveliness. We once had a second assistant director who made a habit of walking into your dressing room just when you had no clothes on. When I asked him to keep people where they couldn't see my tush, his inclination was to bring them closer.

The off-camera scenes often resembled on-camera scenes.

Ellen waiting in
the wings to become
the wisecracking
doctor

The energy expended in fun was deceptive.

This is us figuring out a dramatic moment.

This is us figuring out a comedy scene.

When I didn't know my lines, which was frequently, Loretta would come through the door pointing a finger. Or she would grab me and try to wrestle the lines into my head.

I've always found it difficult to learn words cold off a piece of paper, especially doctor words in Latin and Greek. In the O.R., I would usually be aiming my scalpel at a blood-spattered script. And if you look around Stage 9, you can probably still find scraps of paper, clipboards, and portions of wall with Hawkeye's witicisms neatly printed on them.

The shed (below) became the inner sanctum. It was off-limits to all but the stars of the show. Loretta and Alan used to relax playing a card game called, "Spite and Malice."

We spent a lot of time during our last few days in the shed. The shed was a room that Gary Burghoff had suggested we have made up. It was a tiny room with bare bulbs and raw wooden walls, but it was a place where we could sit between shots and go over our lines together. After a couple of years, the drabness of the place started to get to me and I had fresh flowers delivered every week. The only snag with the shed was that

every night the rats would come in to eat the chrysanthemums and pee on our chess board. We shared the room with some assorted props including bedpans and a couple of bloody dummies that doubled for wounded soldiers.

This (below) was the last read-through of the final MASH script; Writers Thad Mumford and John Rappaport are shown with Bill Christopher and Mike Farrell. (l.r.)

Mike Farrell spent a good part of his time during the final week trying to learn to stand on his hands. It was an interesting example of how we had tried over the 11 years to improve our skills—any skills—no matter how stupid, useless or boring they might be.

Kellye Nakahara (Nurse Kellye) said to
Alan that she grew up on the MASH set.

She went from
being a kid in
her 20's, to
being a woman in
her 30's.
MASH was like
family to her.

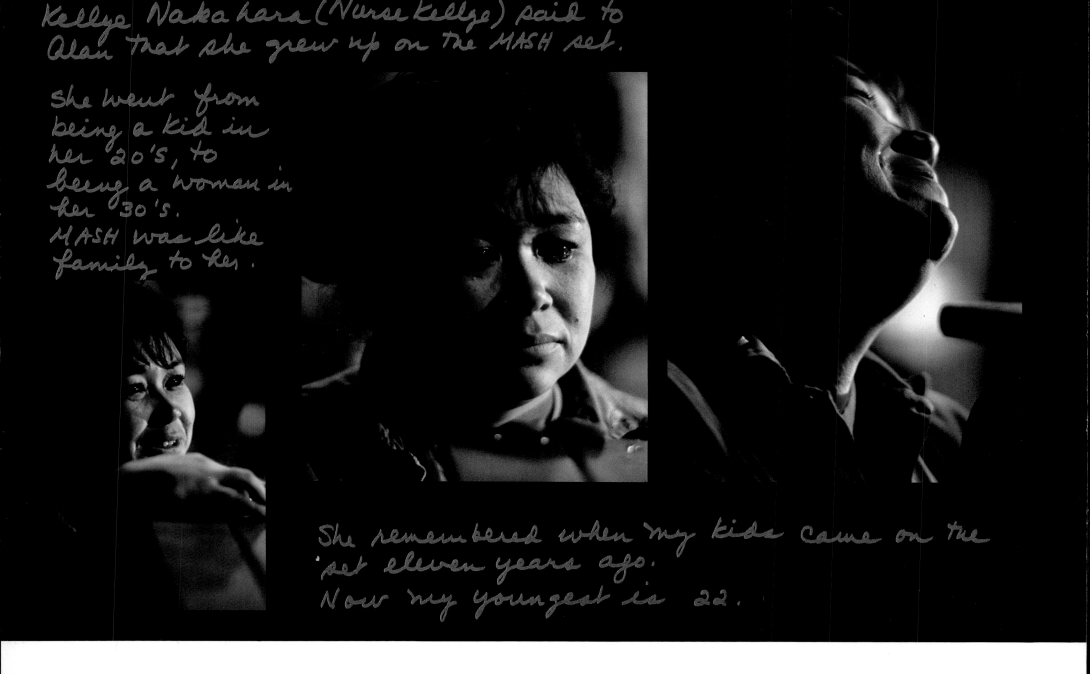

She remembered when my kids came on the
set eleven years ago.
Now my youngest is 22.

The last day.

The nurses on the show sent a surprise balloon bouquet to Rita Bennett, the womens' costumer.

We were overtaken by a sadness that surprised us with its force.

Alan in his dressing room on the last morning.

I kept thinking, "This is the last time I'll do this. The last time I'll wear these clothes. The last time I'll lace these boots."

This was the last time I would say "Good morning" to these people.

We spent all our time in the shed together, partly to go over our lines, but mainly to get away from the crowd of journalists and photographers that was building on the set. Flowers from friends began to fill the room. Mike carried a box of kleenex with him and pretty much used it up.

There were still moments of waiting.
Bill Christopher used some of the
time to read correspondance, with his
real glasses casually put over the
prop glasses he used as Father Mulcahy.
(l.)

Jamie would turn away from you and get out of the room if he saw you were about to get emotional. His moist Mediterranean eyes would fill up and he would look at you and laugh, tears streaming down his face, and say, "Come on. Don't do this to me."

Loretta had the toughest job. She had most of the lines in the final scene in which we buried a time capsule.

Bert Metcalfe, as friend, comforts Loretta during her difficult last scene.

Each time she got to the line, ''And I'm sure each of us hopes that when someone opens this in a hundred years, he or she will know this land was occupied by good, decent—'', it was hard for her not to crack up.

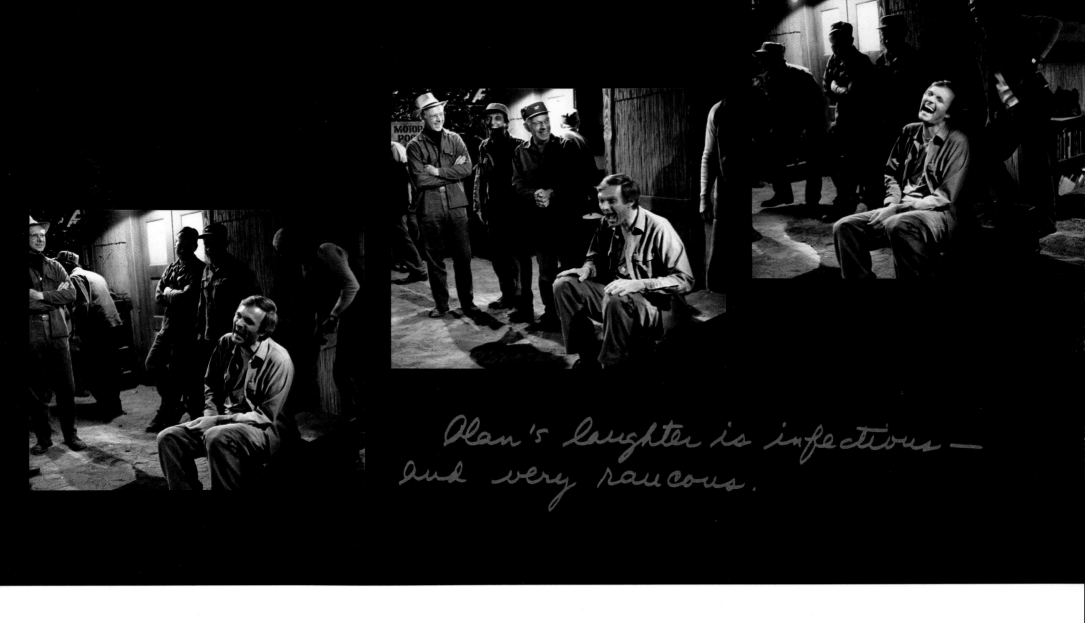

Alan's laughter is infectious—and very raucous.

We needed any release we could find. I sat on a crate and laughed at some filthy ribaldry I can't remember now.

I had a treasured vantage point on a ladder next to the cinematographer. I kept hoping that I wouldn't fall. Climbing ladders isn't fun for me; except when I get a special camera angle.

The tension grew as we all waited for the director's words, "Cut. Print. It's a Wrap."

I didn't fall. I clicked away like crazy.

We did our final shot as 400 people watched and took our picture. I couldn't act. I found it impossible to concentrate. The focus was totally wrong. It felt like being on stage playing to an empty house—with the entire audience watching from the wings.

Burt yelled "Cut" and the final shot was over. Then there was the crush of people. They pushed around us and between us and cut us off from the people we wanted to get to. The private moment we had been looking forward to was lost in a storm of flashing strobes, microphones and video lenses. We went through the motions, numbly.

As far as we know, the burial place of this special box of memorobilia is still very much a secret.

The plans for the burial and the burial itself were carried out in the true MASH spirit; with comraderie, deep feeling, dedication, humor, seriousness, — and a thumbing of noses at the authorities!

All Hail and Farewell.

Arlene Alda

Jamie thought we ought to bury a time capsule of our own. Like kids, we conspired to dig a hole somewhere on the lot at 20th Century Fox. Late at night, we buried a box full of hand props that had become meaningful to us over the years. We lowered the box into its secret grave, covered it with dirt—and laid the show to rest.

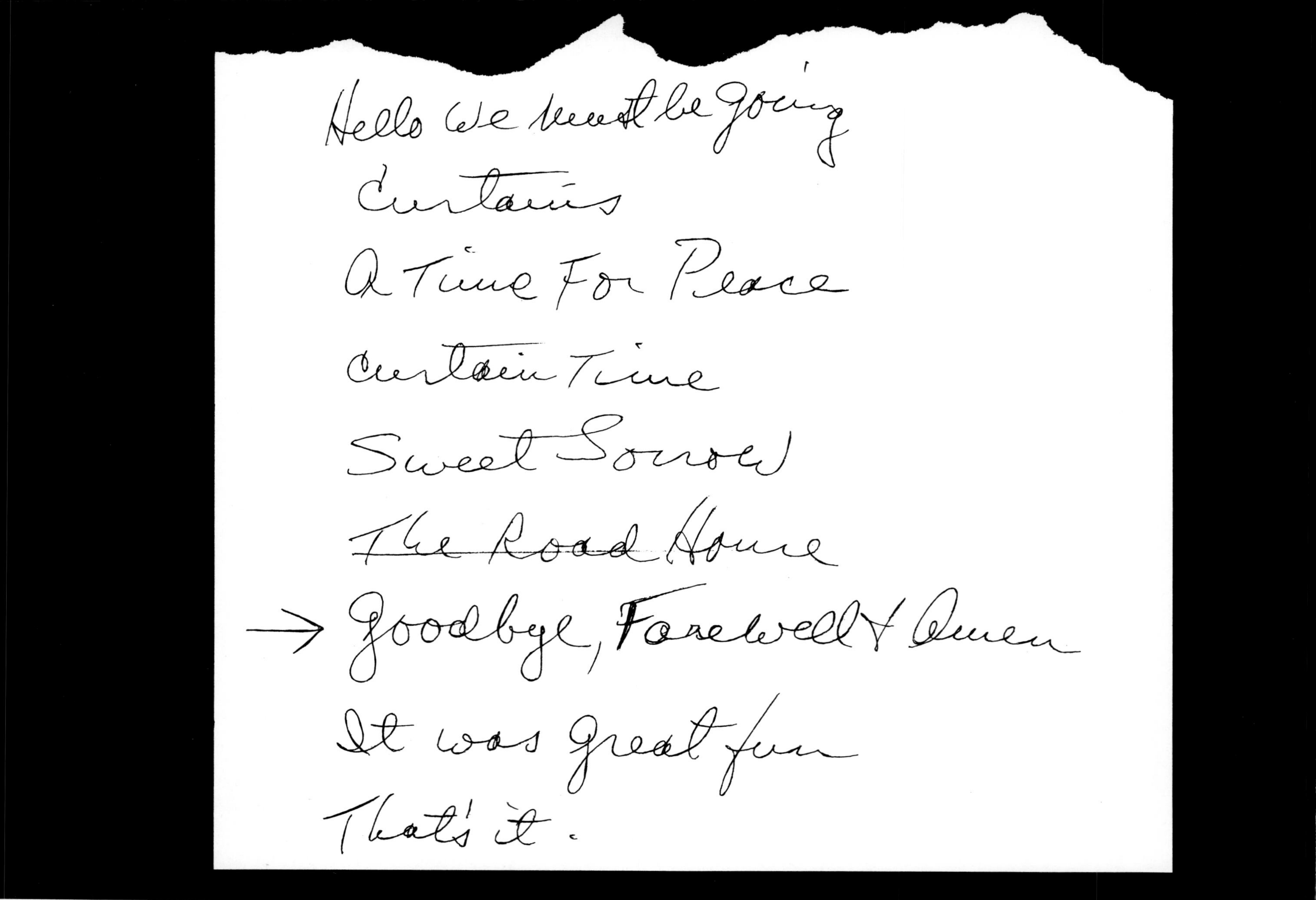

Hello We must be going

Curtains

A Time For Peace

Certain Time

Sweet Sorrow

The Road Home

→ Goodbye, Farewell & Amen

It was great fun

That's it.

I struggled with a lot of title ideas for the movie that would end the series.

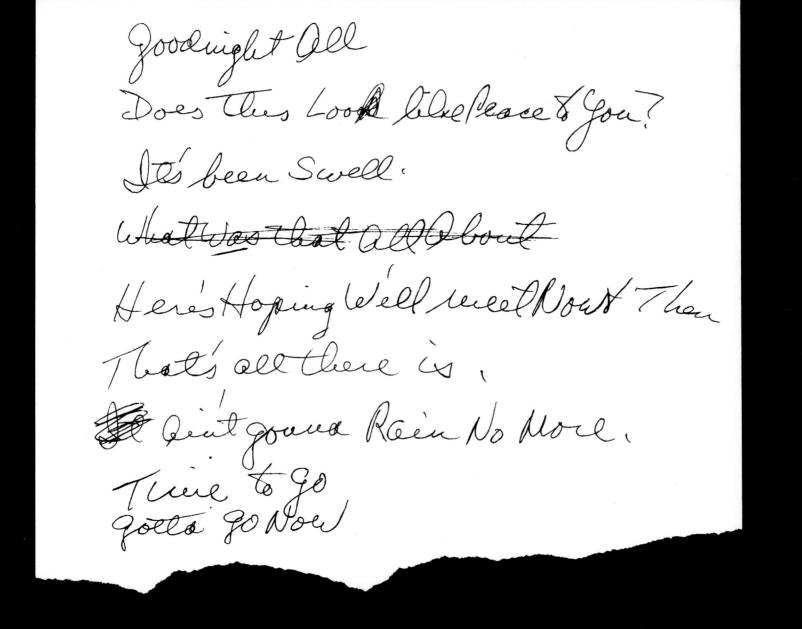

Goodnight All
Does This Look like Peace to You?
It's been Swell.
~~What Was That All About~~
Here's Hoping We'll meet Now & Then
That's all there is.
~~It~~ Aint gonna Rain No More.
Time to go
gotta go Now

For some reason—I guess because he knew how to handle endings with a light touch—I kept coming back to lines from Cole Porter's songs.

SHOOTING SCHEDULE

PROD. NO. __9-B10__	DIRECTOR __BURT METCALFE__
EPISODE __"AS TIME GOES BY"__	UNIT MGR. __DAVID HAWKS__
SHOOTING DATES __JANUARY 10-13, 1983__	ASST. DIR. __CATHY KINSOCK__

DAY/DATE	SETS/SCENES/DESCRIPTION	CAST. & ATMOS.	LOCATION OR STAGE
STAGE 9	INT. CORRIDOR - DAY 1 3/8 Sc. 12 B. J. tells Brannum Stoddard will be okay; Brannum tells Potter Chopper was delayed by engine trouble.	B.J. POTTER BRANNUM STODDARD NURSE #2 1 G.I.	MONDAY 1/10/83 1ST DAY
	INT. OPERATING ROOM - DAY 3/8 Sc. 14 Klinger takes slug that B.J. takes out of Stoddard.	B.J. KLINGER STODDARD NURSE #2 1 Nurse 1 Aneth.	
	INT. POST-OP - DAY 2 Sc. 18 Hot Lips and Hawkeye spat, Stoddard tells them how Brannum saved his life.	HAWKEYE HOT LIPS STODDARD 2 Nurses 6 Patients	
	INT. KLINGER'S OFFICE - DAY 2 Sc. 13 Klinger tries to get Soon-Lee cleared, proffers dress for Hot Lips time capsule and tells her about Hawkeye's. Brannum needs a belt. PROPS: Black Dress	HOT LIPS KLINGER BRANNUM	
	INT. V.I.P. TENT - DAY 2 2/8 Sc. 10 Klinger feeds the imprisoned Soon-Lee; Mulcahy says she'll have to wait for interrogation and that her parents may by nearby. PROPS: Food (Dry) END ACT I	KLINGER MULCAHY SOON-LEE	
	1ST DAY CONTINUED...		

DAY/DATE	SETS/SCENES/DESCRIPTION	CAST. & ATMOS.	LOCATION OR STAGE
STAGE 9	INT. V.I.P. - DAY 1 2/8 Sc. 17 Klinger and Potter free Soon-Lee, as slug from Stoddard doesn't fit her gun. Klinger will take her to depot.	POTTER KLINGER MULCAHY SOON-LEE	MONDAY 1/10/83 1ST DAY (Cont'd.)
	TOTAL PAGES FOR 1ST DAY: 9 2/8		
STAGE 9	INT. MESS TENT - DAY 1 4/8 Scs. 15, 16 Hawkeye takes toast from Igor for his capsule, endures Hot Lips rage. Charles is rude to Rizzo.	HAWKEYE HOT LIPS CHARLES IGOR RIZZO 10 G.I.'s 10 Nurses	TUESDAY 1/11/83 2ND DAY
	INT. OFFICERS' CLUB - NIGHT 3 3/8 Scs. 1,2,3 All discuss time capsule idea; Hot Lips ridicules Hawkeye's offer to help. Rizzo cons Igor out of a dud grenade. PROPS: Hand Grenade	HAWKEYE B.J. HOT LIPS CHARLES IGOR RIZZO G.I.'s Nurses	
	EXT. COMPOUND - NIGHT 2 2/8 Sc. 6 Triage. Corpsman tells Potter Stoddard should be there by now. Potter tells Klinger to incarcerate the prisoner -- Soon-Lee. TRANS: AMBULANCE CAMERA: BL CAMERA	HAWKEYE B.J. POTTER CHARLES KLINGER SOON-LEE NURSE #1 CORPSMAN G.I.'s Nurses 3 Wounded	
	2ND DAY CONTINUED...		

shooting schedule gives advance warning to the cast and crew of the scenes that are to be shot.

DAY/DATE	SETS/SCENES/DESCRIPTION	CAST. & ATMOS.	LOCATION OR STAGE
STAGE 9	EXT. COMPOUND - NIGHT 7/8 Sc. 22 All approach crowded Officer's Club. Charles tosses grenade for guaranteed seating. PROPS: Hand Grenade TAG	HAWKEYE B.J. CHARLES KLINGER SOON-LEE 10 G.I.'s 10 Nurses	TUESDAY 1/11/83 2ND DAY (Cont'd.)
	TOTAL PAGES FOR 2ND DAY: 8		
STAGE 9	INT. SHOWERS - DAY 2 Sc. 8 Rizzo "gets" B.J. with the inert grenade. SPECIAL EFFECTS: Hot water, steam; extra man	B.J. RIZZO	WEDNESDAY 1/12/83 3RD DAY
	INT. SWAMP - DAY 2 6/8 Sc. 19 Charles foils Rizzo's grenade gag by pretending to save Rizzo from the blast. Charles gives high sign to B.J. PROPS: Hand Grenade	B.J. CHARLES RIZZO G.I.'s Nurses	
	INT. SWAMP - DAY 1 4/8 Sc. 9 Hot Lips rejects Charles' offer of a bottle of "booze" for the time capsule; Hawkeye grabs it and follows Hot Lips out of tent.	HAWKEYE HOT LIPS CHARLES G.I.'s Nurses	
	INT. SWAMP - NIGHT 2/8 Sc. 5 Hawkeye, B.J. and Charles are awakened by ambulance and P.A. announcement of Triage. TRANS: Ambulance	HAWKEYE B.J. CHARLES G.I.'s Nurses	
	3RD DAY CONTINUED ...		

DAY/DATE	SETS/SCENES/DESCRIPTION	CAST. & ATMOS.	LOCATION OR STAGE
STAGE 9	INT. POTTER'S TENT - DAY 2 4/8 Sc. 7 All argue about whether Potter should contribute a Zane Grey or a bunion pad to capsule. Klinger reports chopper still missing.	HAWKEYE POTTER HOT LIPS KLINGER	WEDNESDAY 1/12/83 3RD DAY (Cont'd.)
	TOTAL PAGES FOR 3RD DAY: 8 4/8		
STAGE 9	INT. REFUGEE DEPOT - DAY 1 Sc. 20 Mulcahy and Klinger escort Soon-Lee to the couple whom they think are her parents ... they aren't. PROPS: Bowl of Rice	KLINGER MULCAHY SOON-LEE KOREAN WIFE KOREAN HUSBAND 8 Male Refugees 8 Female Refugees 3 Workers (U.N.) 3 Children (Girls) 1 Studio Teacher	THURSDAY 1/13/83 4TH DAY
	EXT. COMPOUND - NIGHT 1 4/8 Sc. 4 Hawkeye will inject irreverance into time capsule; Mulcahy advises refugee couple who are separated from their daughter. TRANSPORTATION: TRUCK	HAWKEYE B.J. HOT LIPS CHARLES MULCAHY KOREAN WIFE KOREAN HUSBAND 3 G.I.'s 5 Nurses 4 Male Refugees 4 Female Refugees	
	PROMOS		
	TOTAL PAGES FOR 4TH DAY: 2 4/8		

s show was filmed in our final week—although it was the next to last show to be aired.

SHOOTING CALL 830A   **CALL SHEET**   DATE MON JAN 10, 1983

PICT. "M*A*S*H"   As TIME GOES BY   NO. 9-B10   DIR BURT METCALFE

SET		SCS.		LOC.
SET INT CORRIDOR (D) (2,3,15,16,17)	SCS. 12		13/8 LOC. STAGE 9
SET INT O.R. (D) (2,6,16,17)	SCS. 14		3/8 LOC.
SET INT POST-OP (D) (1,4,16)	SCS. 18		2 LOC.
SET INT KLINGERS OFC (D) (4,6,15)	SCS. 13		2 LOC.
SET INT VIP TENT (D) (6,7,8)	SCS. 10		2 3/8 LOC.
SET INT VIP TENT (D) (3,6,7,8)	SCS. 17		1 2/8 LOC.
SET		SCS.		LOC.

	CAST AND DAY PLAYERS	PART OF	MAKEUP	SET CALL	REMARKS
1.	ALAN ALDA (NEW)	"HAWKEYE"	10A	1030A	STAGE 9
2.	MIKE FARRELL	"B.J."	8A	830A	MAKEUP DEPT
3.	HARRY MORGAN	"POTTER"	8A	830A	
4.	LORETTA SWIT	"HOT LIPS"	10A	1030A	STAGE 9
5.	JAMIE FARR (NEW)	"KLINGER"	915A	945A	STAGE 9
7.	WILLIAM CHRISTOPHER	"MULCAHY"	230P	3P	
8	ROSALIND CHAO (NEW)	SOON-LEE	230P	3P	
15	MICHAEL SWAN	BRANNUM	745A	830A	MAKEUP DEPT
16	MARK HERRIER	STODDARD	745A	830A	
17	BRIGITTE CHANDLER	NURSE #2	8A	830A	REPORT AS DIRECTED.

CLOSED SET
No VISITORS PLEASE

— ALL CALLS SUBJECT TO CHANGE BY ASSISTANT DIRECTOR. —

ATMOSPHERE AND STANDINS		THRU GATE		
STANDINS		8A		STAGE 9
2 NURSES		9A		
4 PATIENTS		930A		

TUES 1·11·83   STAGE 9   ADVANCE

INT MESS TENT (D) 15,16
INT OFFICERS CLUB (N) 1,2,3
EXT COMPOUND (N) 22,6.

ASST. DIR. C. KINSOCK/B. GELMAN   UNIT PROD. MGR. D. HAWKS

The call sheet comes out daily—naming the scenes to be shot and the equipment and personnel to be used that day.

PRODUCTION REQUIREMENTS

PICTURE "M*A*S*H" As Time Goes By 9-B10 DATE Mon. Jan 10, 1983

	NO.	ITEM	TIME		NO.	ITEM	TIME		NO.	ITEM	TIME
CAMERA	1	CAMERAMAN	8A	**ELECTRICAL**	1	GAFFER	8A	**TRANSPORTATION**		CAMERA TRUCK / SOUND	
	1	OPERATOR			1	BEST BOY				INSERT CAR	
	1	ASSISTANT	✓		4	LAMP OPERATOR	✓		1	STANDBY CAR STN. WAG.	730
	1	ASSISTANT	748A			LOCAL #40 MAN TO:				MOTORHOME (CAST)	
		EXTRA CAMERA			X	HOOK-UP DR. RMS.	7A			GENERATOR	
		EXTRA OPERATOR				OPERATE GENERATOR				BUSSES: MINIVANS	
		EXTRA ASSISTANT				OPERATE WIND MACH.				CREW CAB (TOW WARD.)	
	X	BNCR	748A		X	HEAT STAGE 9	W/N			CAR CARRIER	
	1	KEY GRIP	8A		X	PORTABLE TELEPHONE	7A			JEEPS	
	1	2ND GRIP	(4)		X	SIREN/WIG-WAG				AMBULANCE	
	1	EXTRA GRIPS	✓		X	WORK LIGHTS	✓			EVAC. BUS	
		CRANE & CREW				GAS GENERATOR			X	TRUCKS: GRIP/PROP	S&9
	1	CRAB DOLLY & OPERATOR	748A							WATER WAGONS	
CONSTRUCTION	1	CRAFT SERVICE MAN	730A	**MUSIC**		MUSIC REPRESENTATIVE					
	1	LANDSCAPE MAN	70A			PIANO				SCHOOLROOM TRAILER	
	1	PAINTER				PRACTICAL-DUMMY-TUNE				WARDROBE TRAILER	
	1	PROP. MAKERS	8A			MUSIC TRACKS & CUTTER				HONEYWAGONS (RMS)	
		PLUMBER				P. B.			5	DRESSING RM. TRLRS.	7A
		MECH. EFFECTS MEN						**SOUND**	1	SOUND MIXER	8A
		WARD. CHECK RM.				SIDELINE ORCHESTRA				SOUND RECORDER	
		BENCHES FOR PEOPLE				SINGERS			1	BOOM OPERATOR	8A
		SALAMANDERS							1	CABLE MAN	8A
		PROCESS BODY		**PROCESS**		PROCESS CAMERAMAN				EXTRA CABLE MAN	
		PLYWOOD SCHOOLROOM				PROCESS CAMERA				P. A. SYSTEM	
		PLYWOOD DR. RMS.				PROJ. MACH. & CREW				PLAYBACK MACH. & OPER.	
						STEREO MACH. & CREW				ACETATE REC'DER & OPR.	
		PORTABLE DR. RMS.				PLATES:					
								CAFE		HOT LUNCHES	
MAKEUP	1	MAKEUP MAN	730A	**PROPERTY**	1	PROPERTY MAN	8A			BOX LUNCHES	
		EXTRA MAKEUP MEN			1	ASST. PROP. MAN	✓			DINNERS	
	1	HAIR STYLIST	730A			EXTRA ASST. PROP. MEN			X	GALS. COFFEE	730A
		EXTRA HAIR STYLISTS			1	SET DRESSER	7A			GALS. CHOCOLATE	
		BODY MAKEUP WOMAN			1	LEAD MAN			X	DOZ. DOUGHNUTS	730A
					1	SWING GANG	✓				
		DOORMAN				WARDROBE RACKS		**MISCELLANEOUS**	1	SCRIPT SUPERVISOR	8A
		WARDROBE CHECKER			2	MAKEUP TABLES (LIT)	7A			EXTRA ASST. DIR.	
		WATCHMEN:				BIRDS, ETC.:				STILLMAN	
POLICE		NIGHT DAY				WAGONS, ETC.:				REGISTERED NURSE	
		LOCKER RM. ATTENDANTS:							1	TECHNICAL ADVISOR	8A
		MAN MATRON								MOVIOLA MACHINE	
	1	STUDIO POLICE	730A			HUMANE REPRESENTATIVE				PROJECTIONIST	
		MOTORCYCLE POLICE				WRANGLERS				FILM:	
		POLICE PERMITS				LIVESTOCK:			1	DIALOGUE COACH	8A
										FURN. FOR DRESSING RM.	
WARDROBE	1	COSTUMER (MEN)	7A							FURN. FOR SCHOOL	
	1	COSTUMER (WOMEN)	✓			DEPT. REPRESENTATIVE				FURN. FOR OFFICE	
		EXTRA COSTUMER (MEN)	730A	**PHOTO EFFECTS**							
		EXTRA COSTUMER (WOMEN)				CAMERA		**FIRE**		FIREMAN	
										FIRE WARDEN	

DEPARTMENT	SPECIAL INSTRUCTIONS

ASST DIR C. KINSOCK/B. GELMAN   UNIT PROD. MGR. D. HAWKS

CALL SHEET

5TH DAY OF SHOOTING

SHOOTING CALL 8³⁰A

DATE FRI JAN 14, 1983

PICT. "M*A*S*H" As Time Goes By NO. 9-B10 DIR. BURT METCALFE

SET	SCS.	LOC.
SET	SCS.	LOC.
SET	SCS.	LOC.
SET EXT MOTOR POOL (N)(1,2,3,4,5,6,7, 10)	SCS. 21	3³/₈ LOC. STAGE 9 ✓
SET PRESS CONFERENCE (1,2,3,4,5,6,7)	SCS.	LOC.
SET	SCS.	LOC.
SET	SCS.	LOC.

	CAST AND DAY PLAYERS	PART OF	MAKEUP	SET CALL	REMARKS
1.	ALAN ALDA	"HAWKEYE"	8A	8³⁰A	MAKEUP DEPT
2.	MIKE FARRELL	"B.J."	8A	8³⁰A	
3.	HARRY MORGAN	"POTTER"	8A	8³⁰A	
4.	LORETTA SWIT	"HOT LIPS"	8A	8³⁰A	
5.	DAVID OGDEN STIERS	"CHARLES"	8A	8³⁰A	
6.	JAMIE FARR	"KLINGER"	8A	8³⁰A	
7.	WILLIAM CHRISTOPHER	"MULCAHY"	8A	8³⁰A	
10	G W BAILEY	RIZZO	8A	8³⁰A	

CLOSED SET
ABSOLUTELY NO VISITORS

─ALL CALLS SUBJECT TO CHANGE BY ASSISTANT DIRECTOR─

ATMOSPHERE AND STANDINS	THRU GATE		
3 STANDINS (GOLDMAN, HILL, PETTINGER, THOMPSON, TROY)		8A	STAGE 9
3 GI'S (CLINE, DICKIE, SNIDER)			
5 NURSES (DAVIS, FARRELL, JAY, NAKAHARA, SABA)			

ADVANCE

PRINCIPAL PHOTOGRAPHY COMPLETED
─ END OF 11TH SEASON ─

ASST. DIR. C. KINSOCK/B. GELMAN UNIT PROD. MGR. D. HAWKS

Our last call sheet.

I used the technique of storyboarding when I directed the final movie because there were so many shots to keep track of. A series of simple drawings, a storyboard is a way of visualizing each shot and seeing how it will lead to the next one.

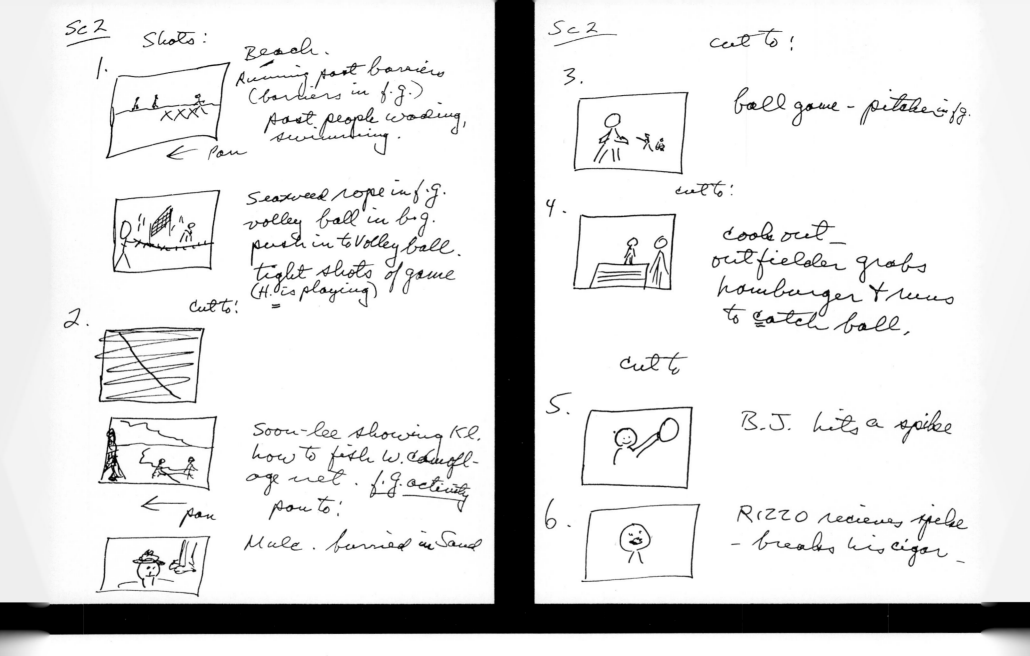

Sc 2   Shots:

1. Beach.
    Running past barriers
    (barriers in f.g.)
    Past people wading,
    swimming.
    ← Pan

    Seaweed rope in f.g.
    volley ball in b.g.
    push in to Volley ball.
    tight shots of game
    (H. is playing)

2.   cut to:

    Soon-lee showing Kl.
    how to fish w. camoufl-
    age net. f.g. activity
    ← Pan   pan to:
    Male. buried in sand

Sc 2   cut to:

3.   ball game - pitcher in f.g.

        cut to:

4.   cook out -
            outfielder grabs
            hamburger + runs
            to catch ball.

        cut to

5.   B.J. hits a spike

6.   RIZZO recieves spike
            - breaks his cigar -

case, the drawings were not only simple, they were crude. But they did allow me to count how m
a set-ups I'd need in each sequence.

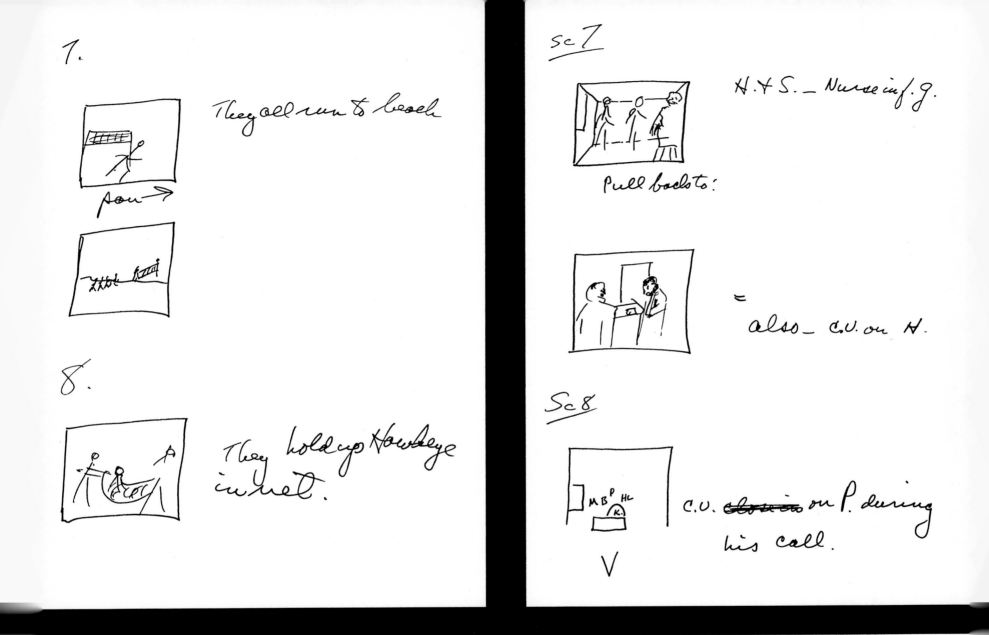

1.

They all run to beach

flow →

8.

They hold up Hawkeye in net.

sc 7

H. & S. — Nurse in f.g.

Pull back to:

also — C.U. on H.

Sc 8

C.U. ~~close in~~ on P. during his call.

V

u remember the movie, (and can figure out these pictures) you'll see that some of these ideas w
n the movie and others didn't. The best laid plans in filmmaking are often just a good bas
ovising.

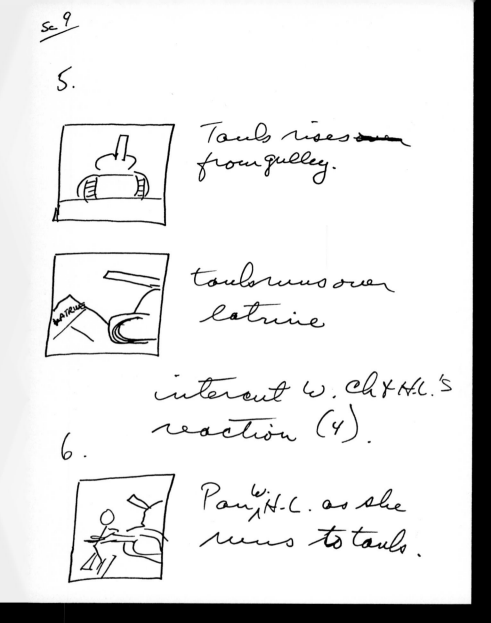

5.

Tank rises ~~over~~
from gulley.

tank runs over
latrine

intercut w. Ch & H.C.'s
reaction (4).

6.

Pan w/ H.C. as she
runs to tank.

(motorcycle)

CH.

Cam. sees ch
emerge fr.
woods — swish pan
to cycle — pull back to
incl. ch & cycle chasing him.

Ch trips on side of road (pad
behind bushes. As they encircle
him, cut in to ch. on ground

ank was shot as I'd planned, but we had to substitute a different tank in later scenes when the firs[t]
[d]estroyed in the fire.

[Scene] 17 with Charles and the cycle had to be completely restaged because the fire took away the wo[ods]
[p]lanned on using.

Sc 19

1.

men working on latrine – stop at sound of music – Rack focus as Potter steps into shot in f.g.

2.

On long lens – Ch in f.g., musicians behind him.
As they cross L to R, they pass people by tents who applaud – (see Ch react)
As they pass VIP tent, BJ comes out.

Sc 35

Mule runs R to L into frame to P.O.W's

Sc 36

Bomb goes off behind Mule. Jeep overturns

Sc 44

Potter on phone
in f.g — —
Kl. enters

Single of P when
he talks to Kl.
=

Let single take us
to two shot of P & Kl
& take them out.

Sc 49

V

→

2 shot of BJ & Sid —
Howie crosses to get cups

BJ crosses into frame
H sits on bed at R. of frame
Cut into singles.
When H rises, he goes
to other bed.

BJ goes to door for Sid.
Sid enters & sits on chair

sc 59

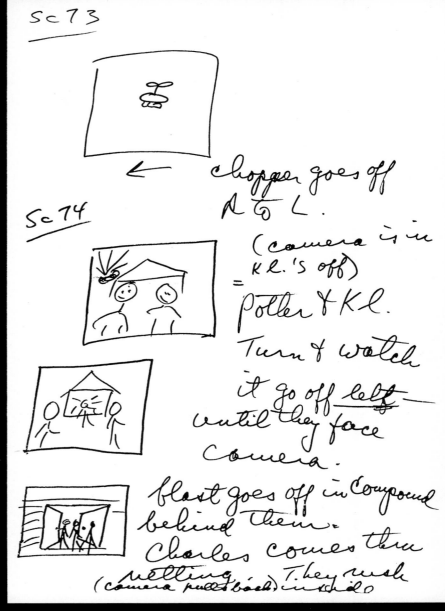

This could be a
still shot —
camera pans
down from
her head to
= baby (head back,
neck limp)
Shoot it both ways

sc 73

sc 74

← chopper goes off
R to L.
(camera is in
KL.'s off)
= Potter & KL.
Turn & watch
it go off left
until they face
camera.

blast goes off in Compound
behind them.
Charles comes thru
yelling. They rush
(camera pulls back) in child

nned the scene with the dead baby two ways. You only have a baby for a few minutes at a time (f
y's protection) so I decided to cover myself. If I couldn't get the baby to hold still long enough t
l, I would pan across a still picture as though the moment were frozen in Hawkeye's memory. It
e been a little too arty that way and I was glad we got a lucky shot of the baby lying still as the c
ned off the mother's grieving face.

Sc 80

MP.
HL
#
CH

(after H.L. enters, push in on Ch & H.L.)

V

open on Ch -
cut to!

chinese musicians

Sc 81

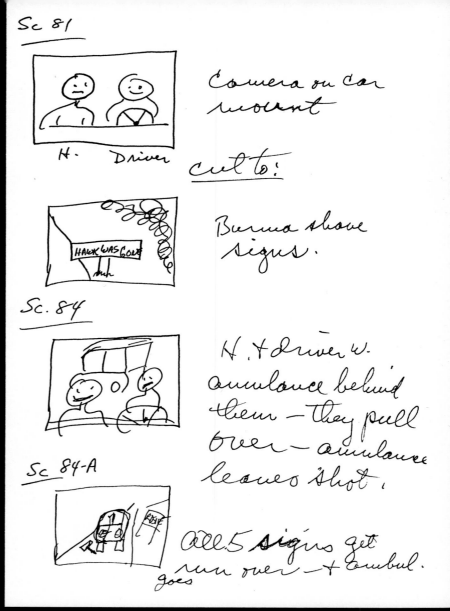

H.   Driver

camera on car mount

cut to!

Burma shave signs.

HAVK WAS GONE

Sc. 84

H. + Driver w. ambulance behind them — they pull over — ambulance leaves shot.

Sc 84-A

ROSE

All 5 signs get run over — + ambul. goes

84-A

Jeep pulls out again as H. looks back at signs

broken signs on ground

Sc 85

POW'S

High shot — arm down as H. gets out of jeep

jeeps

Sc 87   Shoot same day as sc. 63

pan down to

Ch. conducts musicians on side of hill as P. ↓ BJ ~~watch~~ watch

P.   BJ

"The Chinese have been torturing Winch. for a week now."

Sc 98

High Shot –
H. runs fr.
O.R. to Taubtent

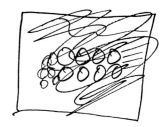

Sc 99.

Sc 100

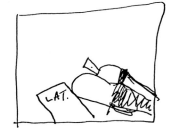

Taub runs over
new latrine –
~~with to~~ dragging tent

Sc 102

we see taub from
rear –
it turns R,
heads for woods

Sc 104

Taub emerges from
woods L to R & plunges
into garbage dumps

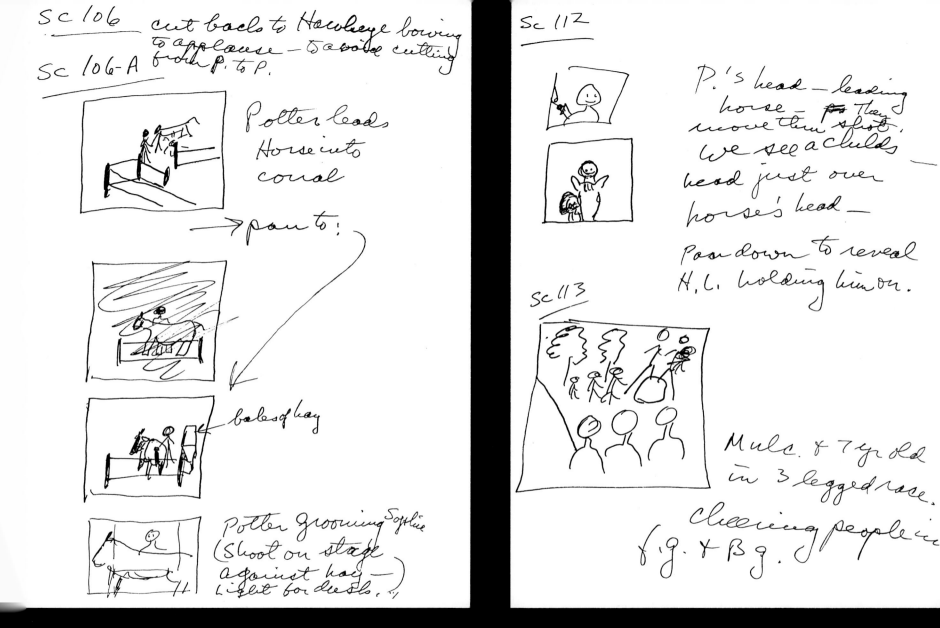

Sc 106　cut back to Hawkeye bowing
to applause — to avoid cutting
Sc 106-A from P. to P.

Potter leads
Horse into
corral

→ pan to:

bales of hay

Potter grooming Softline
(Shoot on stage
against hay —
light for details.)

Sc 112

P.'s head — leading
horse — They
move thru shot.
We see a child's —
head just over
horse's head —
Pan down to reveal
H.L. holding him on.

Sc 113

Mule. & 7 yr old
in 3 legged race.
Cheering people in
f.g. & B.g.

Sc 116, 116A-117

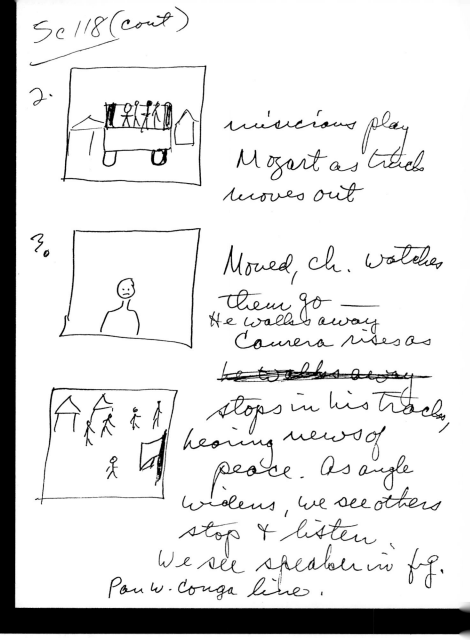

Ch. in bed—
see truck &
musicians
~~the~~ thru
netting.

Ch. ~~g~~ looks,
goes out L.

Sc 118

1.

pan Ch to
truck

Sc 118 (cont)

2.

musicians play
Mozart as truck
moves out

3.

Moved, ch. watches
them go—
He walks away
Camera rises as
~~he walks away~~
stops in his tracks,
hearing news of
peace. As angle
widens, we see others
stop & listen.
We see speaker in fg.
Pan w. conga line.

§,4.

BEST CARE ANYWHERE

Ambulance
pulls in — seen
thru people in g.

Pan w. ~~the~~ Ambul

"we got wounded!"

5.

BJ comes
running
pan him to:

H.L. kneeling
by litter.

"Does this look
like peace to you?"

SC 129

camera dollies to;

dollies more to,

then to!

K SL

SC 129 (cont)

KL & SL.

push then KL.
& S.L. to crowd
pan crowd
til Rizzo cries
then Single of
Mulc —
then:

"I certainly do"
they kiss & crowd
hugs them .

We were surprised and delighted at some of the valentines MASH got from political cartoonists across the country...

Scrod   By Dan DeBellis

Who's who on 'M*A*S*H'

Here's a roster of the 4077th M*A*S*H, past and present:

• **Capt. Benjamin Franklin Pierce, a/k/a Hawkeye (Alan Alda)**, the lynchpin of camp antics but a little insecure behind the fast quip. The kind of guy who, when the 4077th decided to bury a time capsule, decided to contribute a slice of toast.

• **Capt. "Trapper John" McIntyre (Wayne Rogers)**, Hawkeye's irreverent buddy. They share a tent called The Swamp. Rogers left the series in 1975 in a contract dispute.

• **Maj. Margaret Houlihan, a/k/a — in the series' early years — Hot Lips (Loretta Swit)**, chief of nurses at the 4077th. She's comfortable with Army discipline but, like everybody else, needs a little love now and then. Probably the only person in the outfit who would consider pulling rank on a lover.

• **Maj. Frank Burns (Larry Linville)**, nitwit surgeon and Margaret's longtime romantic interest. The kind of guy who would love to have Margaret pull rank on him, Linville left the series in 1977.

• **Corp. Walter "Radar" O'Reilly (Gary Burghoff)**, innocent kid and efficient company clerk. He got his nickname because he could sense when choppers were coming in with the wounded. Burghoff, who left the series in 1979, is the only cast member who played the same role in the movie *M*A*S*H*.

• **Lt. Col. Henry Blake (McLean Stevenson)**, the first C.O. He wants the *M*A*S*H* operating room to be a crack operation, but doesn't much care what the troops do off-duty. Likes a bit of hanky-panky himself. Stevenson left the series in 1975.

• **Father John Mulcahy (William Christopher)**, something of a wimp who often seems out of place. But that's the way it is in the Army—a dash of piety for every gallon of vulgarity.

• **Corp. Maxwell Klinger (Jamie Farr)**, who (in the early years) dresses in women's clothes to prove he's unfit for military service. Pines for the comforts of his hometown, Toledo. But when Radar leaves, Klinger becomes company clerk and hangs up his female outfits.

• **Col. Sherman Potter (Harry Morgan)**, Colonel Blake's successor as commander of the 4077th. A sardonic, salt-of-the-earth father figure who would rather be reading Zane Grey novels than fighting a war.

• **Capt. B.J. Hunnicut (Mike Farrell)**, a surgeon who moves into The Swamp with Hawkeye after Trapper John leaves. Tries hard to ignore the young nurses and stay faithful to his wife.

• **Maj. Charles Emerson Winchester (David Ogden Stiers)**, a character so odd he fits right in at the 4077th. A highbrow Bostonian, but not so high that he'd object to running through the proletariat with Margaret.

—GEORGE BULLARD

Hotlips' kiss worth $522,000

By Jim Bawden Toronto Star

CBS is calling it the most expensive kiss in TV history. For 34.8 seconds, near the conclusion of M*A*S*H's final show Monday night. Hawkeye and Hotlips kissed and kissed. It lasted 34.8 seconds and CBS says since a 30 second commercial cost $450,000, the kiss must be worth $522,000.

If M*A*S*H's overnight ratings are any indication, the finale could become the most watched entertainment program of all time. Final figures aren't expected until after noon.

In New York and Chicago the show reached 72 per cent of the TV audience. In Philadelphia it hit 70 per cent, while in San Francisco it was watched by 82 per cent of viewers.

CBS says the figures put it well ahead of the famous Who Shot J.R.? episode on Dallas which ran in November 1980.

Cast members watched at the screening room on the lot of 20th Century-Fox in Hollywood, then retired to their favorite Moroccan restaurant.

Who Shot J.R.? was watched by 82 million people for 76 per cent of the audience. Roots took 71 per cent and the last Superbowl took 68 per cent of the TV audience.

On the domestic front CTV's U.S. Import, The Winds of War, became the highest rated miniseries on Canadian TV. WOW attracted an average 5.2 million viewers a night and the final installment got 5.9 million. Only the movie Superman surpassed it with 7 million viewers.

Find M*A*S*H drew loyal flush

Flushed with enthusiasm over the final episode of "M*A*S*H," a million New Yorkers apparently waited until the end of the 2½-hour television show before using the bathroom.

Peter Barrett, spokesman for the city Department of Environmental Protection, said yesterday that the water-flow rate increased by 300 million gallons at 11:03 p.m. on Feb. 28, three minutes after the telecast ended. "Engineers who have worked here for 30 or 40 years say they have never seen anything like it before," said Barrett.

He attributed the increased flow to intense interest in the show, which was watched by more than 125 million people nationwide. —**Larry Sutton**

*M*A*S*H Notes for Mozart*

In the last week, WQXR radio has been inundated by New Yorkers calling to ask the name of a certain Mozart piece and to request its airing. The sudden surge of interest in the Quintet for Clarinet and Strings (K. 581) can be traced to the final episode of M*A*S*H, the television comedy about medics in the Korean War, seen last Monday night by 125 million people nationwide. One of the surgeons, a priggish music lover, labored to teach the Western piece to a group of Chinese prisoners of war. Just as the P.O.W.'s were getting the hang of it, they were killed by a bomb.

"There were probably more people hearing Mozart that evening than have ever heard the piece since Mozart wrote it over 200 years ago," said Warren Bodow, executive vice president of the station. WQXR will play the entire quintet Monday at 7:05 P.M.

M*A*S*H Complaints

Sherie Vaughn of Monterey Peninsula TV Cable takes calls from subscribers complaining about being without service, which was disrupted by high winds and rain Monday night during the final episode of M*A*S*H." She offered callers advice on how to set up UHF antennas on their TV sets in order to pick up the signal off the air from KMST-TV, channel 46, which was broadcasting the show.

M*A*S*H F*A*R*E*W*E*L*L

By Mary McGrory

WASHINGTON—OK, take me in, book me, don't bother to read me my rights. I am guilty as charged. It's a clear case of dereliction of duty.

I don't know what the rap is for skipping a dinner where three ex-presidents are speaking in order to watch the finale of "MASH." Maybe you have to do time in Plains in July, or six months of hard labor on Richard Nixon's presidential papers for another installment of his memoirs. Maybe it's caddying for Gerald Ford at the Bob Hope Desert Classic. Whatever the penalty, I will pay it.

If I get to make a speech in the dock, I'll say, for openers, that it will not be "a historic first" —although I do not expect this to keep Nixon from calling it that. Our three former presidents appeared together in public at the funeral of Anwar Sadat.

Even if they hadn't, I will confess that I would have gone ahead with my plans for a counter-dinner. Twelve of us "MASH" heads will eat meatloaf and potatoes, as they do so often in the mess tent—and snow peas in honor of Korea. Then we will wallow in 2½ hours in Ouijongbu in the reviving company of our heroes, who are more real to us than the three survivors of "the splendid misery" of the presidency.

More wit from Hawkeye

Two-thirds of the trio who will be unfolding their napkins three blocks away may not take umbrage—Carter and Ford are "MASH" fans, too—when I say that our group anticipates more wit from Hawkeye, more wisdom from Colonel Potter and more humanity from B.J. Honeycutt than may be dispensed from the head table at the Sheraton-Washington. Nixon probably will; he usually does.

Frankly, it is the auspices of the dinner that I find most liberating. It is in honor of Adm. Hyman Rickover, who exemplifies why a guilt-free evening can be spent out of the presence of people out of office. The admiral, you remember, when it was too late to do any of us any good, told us he was "not proud" of the part he played in building nuclear-powered ships. He would now, when he can no longer do it, "sink them all." Thanks a lot, admiral.

With all due respect, ex-presidents Ford and Carter similarly demonstrate this propensity of public men to say sensible things once they are no longer in a position to put them into effect. Coming back from Sadat's funeral, they boldly informed us that to bring peace in the Middle East, it is necessary to deal with the Palestine Liberation Organization. Neither dared say it in the Oval Office. Ronald Reagan, who would have to face the music from Jewish voters, paid them no mind.

I shall not be there. I shall be at The Swamp, or the O.R., or at Rosie's Bar, or possibly in the supply room with Hawkeye and a new nurse. Wherever I am, I shall be happy in the unseen company of millions of other Americans to whom I do not need to explain my choice. Sure, "MASH" is funny; yes, it is anti-war. But it is much more than that. At the 4077th, as distinct from Washington, people speak their minds and feelings and make tremendous progress in understanding themselves and one another.

Hawkeye goes to surgery drunk. He leaves an operation in mid-course. He commits the sacrilege of screaming at the adoring, wounded Radar. No one excuses him. They line up to tell him off, even gentle Father Mulcahy. Hawkeye knows he has been a jerk. He reconciles with Radar as an equal. He gives Radar his beer; he takes Radar's Nehi grape.

The romantic message of "MASH" is that people can accept help in the form of home truths about themselves, which, of course, in real life is not always the case. It is as much the constant, successful transactional analysis as the wise-cracks that give the show its therapeutic content. It goes on even when the Dr. Sidney Freeman—Hawkeye calls him "the skull jockey" —is not in. Everyone does it. Hawkeye's back is killing him. Colonel Potter tells him he is crippled with anger at a doctor back home who is making hay while Hawkeye stews and fumes in the Swamp. Hawkeye straightens up.

People always grow and improve on "MASH." Maj. Margaret Houlihan is transformed from a banshee to a woman before our eyes. Toledo-crazed Klinger became responsible. "MASH" is telling us that it's too bad that the triumph of human decency doesn't occur more often outside a war zone.

I throw myself on the mercy of the court.

Mish-'M*A*S*H': A quiz for the aficionado

By Amy Parrent
News Special Writer

You claim you moved to a town where M*A*S*H is shown three times every weekday just so you could watch it 16 times a week (including Monday nights)? You say if there can be such a thing as a (Star) Trekkie, then you're a M*A*S*Hie? You modestly reveal you've seen all 250 M*A*S*H episodes shown so far? And tomorrow night, if Queen Elizabeth wanted to visit your house you'd say, "Wait till Tuesday, Liz, baby. I've got to see the big M*A*S*H finale." Well then, M*A*S*Hie, this quiz is for you. (Each correct answer is worth one point, unless otherwise noted.)

I. THESE PEOPLE HAVE CHARACTER

1. What is Hawkeye's full, real name?
2. Charles Winchester's middle name is?
A. Emerson
B. Ogden
C. Remington
3. Who is William Christopher?
4. This M*A*S*H guest star played a Swedish doctor named Inga:
A. Mariette Hartley
B. Liv Ullmann
C. Pia Lindstrom
D. Pia Zadora
5. Klinger's ancestors came from what country?
6. List the two male relatives of Alan Alda who've appeared on M*A*S*H. (2 points)
7. Harry Morgan's first appearance on M*A*S*H was as:
A. Col. Potter
B. A crazy general
C. A policeman
D. Klinger's father, who was touring the base as a USO girl.

8. The radio operator at another base whose name is often mentioned is called:
A. Phones
B. Billy
C. Sparky
9. What is one of Frank Burns' nicknames?
A. Thin Lips
B. Thick Head
C. Ferret Face
D. Bette Davis Eyes

II. THE PLOT THICKENS

1. Over the years on M*A*S*H, several major characters have left. Match these characters with the reasons given for their departure. (3 points)
A. Henry Blake
B. Frank Burns
C. Radar
1. Had enough service points
2. Started going crazy while on leave
3. A relative died; he was needed at home
2. Margaret Houlihan once had a brief romantic involvement with which one of these men:
A. Col. Flagg
B. Radar
C. Hawkeye
D. B.J.
3. In one episode the other leading players got revenge on Charles by cleaning him out in a poker game. What did he do every time he had a bad hand that tipped them off he was bluffing?
A. He whistled loudly
B. He tapped his feet
C. He burped
D. He rubbed his tummy and patted his head
4. What's the name of the nearby off-base bar the M*A*S*H gang visits?
A. The Lindell A.C.
B. The Chinese Tea Room
C. S*M*A*S*H*E*D
D. Rosie's

5. B.J.'s wife organized a party for the M*A*S*H unit's stateside families. What did Charles's parents do at the party which upset him when he heard about it later?
A. They drank out of the fingerbowls
B. They wore lampshades on their heads
C. They stayed at the Y instead of the Waldorf
D. They invited Radar's family to visit them in Massachusetts after the war

III. YOU'D KNOW THEIR FACES ANYWHERE

1. What type of doctor is Major Sidney Freedman?
A. Gynecologist
B. Podiatrist
C. Ear, Nose, Throat
D. Psychiatrist
2. What role does actress Kellye Nakahara play?
3. What character does actor Jeff Maxwell play?
A. Arnie
B. Edgar
C. Igor

IV. THE ACTORS' RESUMES

1. Harry Morgan was formerly a featured player on:
A. *Bonanza*
B. *Dragnet*
C. *Saturday Night Live*
D. *Pink Lady and Jeff*
E. *Hello, Larry*
2. In a 1960's Broadway musical called *The Apple Tree*, Alan Alda played:
A. Adam (the first man)
B. William Tell
C. One of the Andrew sisters
3. Which of these has never directed an episode of M*A*S*H for television?
A. Mike Farrell
B. Jackie Cooper

C. Alan Alda
D. Robert Altman
4. What other current CBS show had a "pilot" movie which starred Loretta Swit?
A. *The Dukes of Hazzard*
B. *Cagney and Lacey*
C. *Alice*
D. *Newhart*
5. In what musical based on a famous comic strip did Gary Burghoff star during the 1960s?
A. *You're a Good Man, Charlie Brown*
B. *You're Quite a Lady, Lois Lane*
C. *You're a Bad Dog, Marmaduke*
D. *Annie*

V. ON THE HOME FRONT

1. What is Hawkeye's hometown in Maine?
2. B.J. is from:
A. Houston, Tex.
B. Boston, Mass.
C. Mill Valley, Calif.
D. Seattle, Wash.
3. Radar is from:
A. Ottumwah, Iowa
B. Butte, Mont.
C. Gary, Ind.
D. Huzzah, Mo.
4. What is B.J.'s wife's name? What is his daughter's name (2 points)
5. What did Margaret's father do for a living?
A. Oilman
B. Career Army man
C. Hospital administrator
D. Owned Frederick's of Hollywood
6. What is Charles's sister's name?
A. Honoria
B. Winnie
C. Muffy
D. Sneezy
E. Dopey

Feeling blue about M*A*S*H?

In living rooms throughout our area as well as across the country Monday night, there wasn't a dry eye to be found. There on the TV screen was the last hurrah of M*A*S*H, bowing out after an 11 year run, finally sending home Hawkeye, B.J., Klinger and the rest of the 4077th.

If you're feeling blue about the loss of your favorite friends on the Korean front, you're not alone. According to NYU Medical Center psychiatrist Dr. Robert London "the general viewing audience will feel a tremendous disappointment when M*A*S*H finally goes off the air. It was a quality program that showed the paradoxes of war and at the same time allowed us to laugh at ourselves." The head of the short-term psychotherapy unit at NYU also credited the show with being one of the few popular culture creations in recent history to touch "real feelings."

London predicted emotional withdrawal symptoms for some segments of the population and suggested that watching re-runs may ease their sense of loss and unhappiness. Given the low level of general programming, however, he warns the networks that if they continue to underestimate popular taste and intelligence, "viewers will become increasingly angry and disenchanted with commercial TV and begin to seek other outlets for their leisure time."

Which, when you think about it, isn't such a bad idea.

Great Neck Record

'MASH' Farewell Tops Old Records

Monday's "MASH" finale grabbed a 60.3 Nielsen rating, easily the highest rating ever for a single program, topping the "Who Shot J.R.?" episode of Dallas by a full 7 points.

And CBS Research estimates the "MASH" farewell attracted an audience of 125,000,000 U.S. viewers, shattering the previous single-program record by about 26,000,000. That mark was set last Jan. 30 by the Super Bowl telecast on NBC.

For the night, "MASH" boosted CBS' primetime average to a 55.4 rating, 71 share, crushing the ABC (9.6/12) and NBC (8.1/10) opposition. The NBC rating tied as the season's lowest average and the ABC rating was the fifth lowest.

The current list of highest rated single programs in tv history is headed by "MASH" (60.3/77), "Dallas" (53.3/76), the concluding episode of "Roots" (51.1/71), Super Bowl 16 (49.1/73) and Super Bowl 17 (48.6/69).

Variety

Answers to M*A*S*H quiz

I.
1. Benjamin Franklin Pierce
2. A.
3. The actor who portrays Mulcahy.
4. A.
5. Lebanon.
6. His father, Robert, and his brother, Anthony.
7. B.
8. C.
9. C.

II.
1. A-1; B-2; C-3.

2. C.
3. A.
4. D.
5. D.

III.
1. D
2. She plays the nurse called Kellye.
3. C.

IV.
1. B.
2. A.
3. D.
4. B.
5. A.

V.
1. Crabapple Cove.
2. C.
3. A.
4. His wife's name is Peg. His daughter's name is Erin.
5. B.
6. A.

SCORING
25-33 points. You win a two-day pass to South Korea's largest city (does this make you a Seoul brother?).

18-24. You win a "Men of M*A*S*H nude calendar (with Klinger as MR. JANUARY wearing only a garter belt).

10-17. If you didn't know the plots, you probably only watch Channel 50 re-runs— they make more cuts than Sweeney Todd.

Below 10. The Army would describe your answers as "Fouled Up Beyond All Recognition."

The News

M*A*S*H a S*M*A*S*H as Museum Show

By GAIL MILGRAM

Washington

Feb. 28, 1983, was a big day in American history. Not only did the Korean War end for the second time, but two inseparable surgeons named Hawkeye and B.J. parted company, their friend Klinger got married and their nemesis Winchester deliberately smashed a Mozart record—all in 2½ hours. In an episode called "Goodbye, Farewell, and Amen," M*A*S*H finally came to an end after 11 years at the forefront of prime-time television.

Or so we thought. But in fact it will be another year before the officers' tent is dismantled and Klinger's wardrobe is condemned to the mothballs. Until Sept. 30, 1984, sets, costumes and other memorabilia from the series will be on display in a retrospective exhibit that already has broken all attendance records at the Smithsonian's National Museum of American History in Washington.

Since M*A*S*H: Binding Up the Wounds" opened on July 30, crowds of eager visitors have been gathering every morning outside the museum's entrance on the Mall near the Washington Monument. When the doors open at 10 a.m., they rush past the prominently displayed original Star-Spangled Banner to get free passes that specify at what time they can view the M*A*S*H exhibit. Then they all have to wait their turns, sometimes for three or four hours.

Fortunately, boredom is hardly a problem in the Museum of American History, which collects anything and everything that has ever been a part of American culture. Extensive assortments of rare musical instruments, clocks and firearms are on display, as are a selection of First Ladies' gowns and a film montage of well-known sports figures. An authentic 19th-century schoolroom brought intact from Cleveland helps illustrate the development of American education, while a '30s kitchen, complete down to the cereal boxes, reflects the life style of immigrants between the world wars. After a quick look at Judy Garland's red shoes from "The Wizard of Oz," M*A*S*H fans can spend the last few minutes of their wait staring in disbelief at a 12-ton, half-nude statue of an enthroned George Washington—one of the few reminders around that Washington's head was once attached to the rest of him.

The M*A*S*H retrospective is very much in line with the museum's other exhibits. Seen together, its various parts show how Americans in the 1970s confronted sensitive social and political issues with an unprecedented frankness and sophisticated humor.

Alan Alda as Hawkeye

And when the exhibit ends next year, these same items will contribute substantially to the museum's military-history, medical-sciences and popular-entertainment collections.

The M*A*S*H exhibit occupies only a few yards of wall space in front of George Washington, but it takes a good half hour to absorb all the materials and their footnotes. The visitors snaking through in single file are so busy trying to digest this exegesis of their favorite television comedy that no one seems to mind the slow pace.

First on display is a series of photographs comparing the M*A*S*H 4077th to the 8055th MASH, its real Korean War counterpart. The parallels are striking, and it turns out that costumes and sets for the program were researched so extensively that they really do provide a remarkably accurate documentation of conditions in the Korea of the early 1950s. Immediately following the photographs are the complete sets for the 4077th's operating room and for the officers' tent that Hawkeye jokingly called the Swamp. Both are more primitive than they ever looked on the screen, and knowing that they represent reality makes them seem that much more gruesome and claustrophobic.

But most visitors seem more interested in the M*A*S*H characters themselves than in historical accuracy. "What I liked best about the show was its human quality," said one woman. "The characters were real people with real senses of humor." Others are more impressed by the political thrust of the series, which began its long run toward the end of the Vietnam War. "The show was more than just good entertainment, because it dealt with important issues during a very difficult period of our history," said a man in his late 20s. "Its anti-war statement reached so many people."

The last section of the exhibit, which is meant to illustrate the importance of M*A*S*H in entertainment history, is like a miniature Tinseltown Museum. The first and second drafts of the show's pilot script are there, along with photographs of the actors, Hot Lips' clipboard, Hawkeye's boots and two of Klinger's most fetching costumes, worn before him by Betty Grable and Ginger Rogers.

If M*A*S*H enthusiasts have not had enough after this, they can go to the Army supply tent recently installed in the museum's lobby and buy their own M*A*S*H dog tags, T-shirts and helmets, or a teddy bear just like Radar's. Of course, there is always the new series airing this fall, AfterMASH, which reunites Father Mulcahy, Klinger and Col. Potter. And if that is still not enough, three M*A*S*H reruns a night for a couple of years should do the trick.

Ms. Milgram writes frequently on cultural subjects.

Telegram

western union

RONALD REAGAN
    THE WHITE HOUSE, WASHINGTON, D.C.

THE M.A.S.H CAST

DEAR FRIENDS:

NANCY AND I WELCOME THE OPPORTUNITY TO
EXTEND OUR GREETINGS TO ALL WHO GATHER
FOR THE M.A.S.H WRAP PARTY

THIS IS A SPECIAL NIGHT FOR ALL OF YOU
AND WE KNOW HOW PROUD YOU MUST BE OF
YOUR SUCCESS.

        RONALD REAGAN

GERALD R. FORD
    RANCHO MIRAGE, CALIFORNIA

MASH CAST AND CREW

CONGRATULATIONS TO ALL OF THE MASH CREW
ON PRODUCING FOR ALL OF US SO MANY YEARS
OF THE VERY FINEST IN ENTERTAINMENT.
I'VE ALWAYS BEEN A MASH LOVER, SO I'M
SADDENED BY THE NEWS OF THE LAST DAY OF
SHOOTING. I HOPED IT WOULD NEVER END.
GOOD LUCK AND GOD BLESS EACH OF YOU.

WARMEST BEST WISHES

        JERRY FORD

western union Mailgram

FROM JIMMY CARTER
    ATLANTA, GEORGIA

TO THE STAFF, CAST, CREW OF M*A*S*H

IT IS WITH MUCH REGRET THAT I WISH YOU
ALL FAREWELL. I THANK YOU FOR PROVIDING
THE NATION WITH ELEVEN YEARS OF TALENT
AT ITS FINEST. YOU HAVE SUCCESSFULLY
RENDERED AN AMERICAN PORTRAIT,
HIGHLIGHTED BY COMIC SATIRE, AND WE WHO
LOVE AND HONOR ALL THAT OUR COUNTRY
REPRESENTS APPRECIATE THE RESULTS YOU
HAVE ACHIEVED. YOURS HAS BEEN A GIFT OF
WISDOM AND HUMOR COMBINED, AND WE HAVE
ALL BEEN GREATLY ENTERTAINED. WE WILL
MISS YOU.

                JIMMY CARTER

HENRY A. KISSINGER
    WASHINGTON, D.C.

TO THE MASH CAST AND TEAM

I AM RELIEVED TO LEARN THAT PEACE IS AT
HAND, FINALLY, IN THE KOREAN WAR.

NEVERTHELESS, I JOIN YOUR MILLIONS OF
FANS IN REGRETTING THE END OF SUCH A
BRILLIANTLY SUCCESSFUL SHOW,
CONGRATULATIONS ON AN OUTSTANDING
ACHIEVEMENT.

BEST REGARDS

                HENRY A. KISSINGER

WILLIAM S. PALEY
   CBS, NEW YORK, NEW YORK

MR. ALAN ALDA

THE FINAL EPSIODE OF MASH NOT ONLY WAS
SUPERB IN ITSELF, BUT ALSO PROVIDING A
TRIUMPHANT AND POIGNANTLY FITTING
CONCLUSION TO A SERIES WHICH HAS DONE
HONOR TO HISTORY OF TELEVISION. THE
EXTRAORDINARY NATIONAL OUTPOURING OF
ENTHUSIASM AND AFFECTION MONDAY EVENING
WAS A RICHLY DESERVED TRIBUTE TO THE
PHENOMENAL EXTENT TO WHICH YOU AND YOUR
COLLEAGUES HAVE TOUCHED THE HEARTS OF
YOUR AUDIENCE. YOU AND THE MASH FAMILY
ON BOTH SIDES OF THE CAMERA HAVE BROUGHT
NEW DIMENSIONS TO THE ART OF TELEVISION.
I HOPE YOU WILL TELL THE REST OF THEM,
FOR ME, HOW MUCH I ADMIRE THERE
CONSISTENT EXCELLENCE. WE AT CBS ARE
PROUD TO HAVE BEEN THE NETWORK THAT MADE
MASH A PART OF THE AMERICAN EXPERIENCE.
THE NEXT TIME YOU ARE IN NEW YORK I HOPE
YOU WILL LET ME KNOW, SO WE CAN GET
TOGETHER. MEANWHILE, MANY THANKS AND
BEST WISHES TO YOU AND ALL OF YOUR
ASSOCIATES.

                BILL PALEY
                (FOUNDER CHAIRMAN - CBS)

MAX CLELAND, SECRETARY OF STATE -- GEORGIA
   ATLANTA, GEORGIA

TO THE CAST, THE STAFF AND THE CREW OF
M.A.S.H

CONGRATULATIONS ON THE COMPLETION OF ONE OF
THE MOST OUTSTANDING PROGRAMS IN THE HISTORY
OF TELEVISION. AS MY OWN LIFE WAS SAVED BY
MEDICAL PERSONNEL WORKING OUT OF A QUANSET
HUT, I AM PARTICULARLY GRATEFUL FOR THE
EXCELLENT JOB YOU HAVE DONE IN BRINGING
INSIGHT INTO THE CONTRIBUTION AND SACRIFICE
MADE BY MILITARY MEDICAL PERSONNEL ON THE
BATTLEFIELD. BEST OF LUCK TO ALL OF YOU IN
THE FUTURE; COUNT ME IN ON THE MASH TEAM.

                MAX CLELAND
                (FORMER ADMINISTRATOR --
                VETERANS ADMINISTRATION)

American Saddlebred Horse Association, Inc.

929 South Fourth Street • Louisville, Kentucky 40203

OFFICIAL CERTIFICATE OF REGISTRATION

This is to Certify, that _____ a Stallion _____ has been duly registered in **The American Saddlebred Horse Association's Register** and the pedigree can there be traced in the following form.

Owned by **W.L. Nininger**
P. O. **Bristol, Virginia**
Bred by **Owner**
P. O. _____

Sire **Society's Beau Brummell**
Reg. No. **55172**

Reg. No. **77273**
Name of this Entry

HAWKEYE PIERCE

Dam **Shy Valley April Shower**
Reg. No. **73038**

Sex **Stallion** Color **Chestnut**
Markings **Small star, left front ankle, right front, left hind pasterns, white.**
Foaled **May 27, 1981**

Pedigree

- **Daring Society 48448** (GRANDSIRE)
  - By **Hickory Society Rex 43707**
    - By **Society Rex 15454**
    - **Kate Shriver 43606**
  - **Daring Shy Ann 41072**
    - By **Nawbeek's Highland King 19021**
    - **Daring Glory 29087**
- **Dogwood Blossom 53319** (SIRE'S DAM)
  - By **American Victory 21563**
    - By **Nawbeek's Highland King 19021**
    - **Hazel Love 15690**
  - **Lucky May 27862**
    - By **Todd's Val Jean 15833**
    - **Lena Walford 15863**
- **Ridgefields Fancy 44914**
  - By **Anacacho's Captain Denmark 38955**
    - By **Anacacho Denmark 16033**
    - **Belle Of Boyle 31444**
  - **Gene Doris 53548**
    - By **Ridgefield's Genius 22806**
    - **Anne Doris 35394**
- **Bay Rocket 61184** (2nd DAM)
  - By **Red Ace 39143**
    - By **Sun O'Gun 12954**
    - **June Breeze 37645**
  - **Miss Trousdale 51889** (3rd DAM)
    - By **Sun O'Gun 12954**
    - **Dipsy Doodle's Sweetheart 39862** (4th DAM)

Given under my hand and seal, at Louisville, Kentucky, this **10th** day of **November** A.D. **1981**

Charles J. Cromwell Jr.
Authorized Officer

"I am an American Serviceman serving in the US Army in Korea. I am stationed at the 121st Evacuation Hospital at Seoul.

In Korea, the M*A*S*H television shows we get are at least 6 months old, but still everyone watches everyone of them.

I am writing this letter to inform you of the fate of Rosie's Bar at Uijongbu, Korea. Some years ago the original Rosie moved to the United States, but her daughter continued to operate Rosie's Bar. Due to the US Troop withdrawals, the Army compound located near Rosie's Bar was deactivated and turned over to the Korean Army. This loss of US personnel sealed the fate of Rosie's Bar. With the loss of income from the US Servicemen, Rosie's Bar closed. Rosie's daughter now moved to the United States to be with her mother. So ends the tale of Rosie's Bar.

Just thought you might like to know about the real Rosie's Bar."

"As February 1983 approaches and the reality of MASH having a final episode actually strikes, I am finally motivated to write my first letter ever to the cast of a television show. This letter has been written many times in my mind but never have I been able to commit it to paper. Even though I am now writing it, the possibility of your ever seeing it still seems remote. However . . . here it goes.

As a Vietnam Veteran, I have been able to 'feel' your shows as well as enjoy them. Korea or Vietnam . . . what's the difference? During these past ten years when our Country was silent about the Vietnam War, your show gave me comfort. Somebody understood. Somebody was expressing what war 'really is'."

"During the last decade you and the fine people who make up MASH have treated me to a (thank goodness) gradual understanding of how my Dad survived his tour of duty as a surgeon during the Korean police action. Bits of Dad surfaced during the saga of MASH -- the purple heart won by ineptitude, terrific teller of tales, the man who got the penicillin to the orphanage -- the stock-in-trade of many childrens' memories, I'm sure.

Thanks for spreading him out over so many characters. B.J., Hawkeye, and Father Mulcahey come too close, each in his own way.

I think Dad came back from Korea with his ethics doing overtime. At 67, he still makes house calls."

"My husband is a Vietnam Vet. From watching MASH over the last 10-11 years, your manner of dealing with war - through humor - has made a tremendous difference in acting as a pressure relief valve for my husband's emotions of hurt and pain from the horror of war.

You and the entire staff have been the best psychiatrist my husband could have ever had to deal with the aftershock of Vietnam."

"Tonight, along with many millions of other Americans, my wife and I viewed the Sayonara Program of M A S H. I would not be true to my own emotions if I failed to express two thoughts in appreciation.

First, that of deep gratitude to you and to each member of your cast for eleven years of entertainment which allowed me to relive many experiences and relationships of my own military career (1941--1967) as a chaplin - US Army and Airforce. I know what it is to trust, respect, and love those having a common mission and spirit of dedication. I, too, said my farewells in the Pacific, in Germany, in Japan, Korea, and many stateside Bases. M A S H's farewells were far more than entertainment. I have learned to appreciate Major Winchester -- a wee bit.

Second, the absence of M A S H leaves a great void in quality TV Programing. I believe that most viewers, contrary to the judgment of some in high places, still appreciate having a choice between the sordid and the wholesome. I have heard you speak at Award Programs and on Talk Shows. Please do what you can Mr. Alda, to assure that American Youth, and millions of Senior Citizens continue to have that opportunity of choice."

"I am writing to thank you for 'The War Is Over.' This episode, and many other episodes, had a very special meaning to me. I am a Veteran of the war in Vietnam, not a casualty, a Veteran. Today I lead a normal middle-class life. In some ways you all helped me to do that.

During the program when it was broadcast over the PA system that the war was over I stood and cheered. For you see, to me and probably many other Vets, we had never been able to do that. Like your presentation of the casualties after the ceasefire we had many more wounds and wounded to tend to. And this night we had a celebration marking the end of the war. You gave us that big moment that we had never had."

"Please find enclosed a copy of our church's bi-monthly newsletter. After the final show of M*A*S*H I tried to put into words why the show has meant so much to me over the last decade.

Thanks for all the laughter and thoughts you and M*A*S*H have brought me and many others."

G R A C E   F I L L E D   M O M E N T S

March 20, 1983 - April 2, 1983

SAYING GOODBYE!

"Well, it finally happened. I knew deep inside that the time would come, but I simply wasn't ready for it. After 11 years, part of me went as well. M*A*S*H is no more (except for re-runs). I cried through over 50 percent of its 2 1/2 hour long farewell.

I've tried to analyze why I care so much about this show. Partially, it is because of the fact that drivel is the rule rather than the exception on modern TV that M*A*S*H is such a shining star. Also, a lot of the escapism that is presented keeps us focused away from our own problematic realities. But, M*A*S*H plugged me into the dreariest, most depressing of events - Reality. It made reality fun or at least bearable. Hawkeye, the consummate smart aleck, helps me justify my own smart aleck streak.

Hawkeye and B.J. each had something about them that I would like to have. Hawkeye's making fun of life helped life go down a little easier and helped me take myself a little less seriously. B.J.'s calmness in the face of most any tragedy reminded me of Who is in charge and is a trait I'd like to call my own.

In essence, M*A*S*H, was more of a church than a hospital. The characters were human. They cared and erred, they had clay feet and compassionate hearts, they had smart mouths and sensitive souls. They were a family, sometimes more, sometimes less like the family of God. To me, they were a symbol of hope in the midst of tragedy, caring in the midst of the ultimate injustice, Life in the midst of death."

M*A*S*H--Goodbye, Farewell, and Amen!

"As a senior at Canton Agricultural and Technological College in Canton, New York, I do not find much time to watch television, but have always managed to put my work aside to watch M*A*S*H.

I live in an apartment complex of two hundred college students as tenants, who are usually playing stereos, yelling or running around. The night the final episode of M*A*S*H aired, there was almost complete silence for two and a half hours. I guess that tells you, people really wanted to listen to and remember the ending episode, the end of the Korean War.

I will always remember, Hawkeye Pierce, and other cast members after the re-runs aren't shown anymore, in twenty years or so. I think I learned more about the Korean War through watching M*A*S*H then from any teacher's lecture given or book read."

"The operating room scenes were such a tension relief for us, who work in a hospital where sterile technique in the O.R. is a must.

We sisters, all had our favorites - you, B.J. Farrell, Winchester, Potter, Radar, etc. etc. and we would like to have 'Hot Lips' on our staff to handle some of our doctors!

We wish you and your co-workers the best in real life, and may all of you be blessed with good health, good marriages and a good future.

God bless each one of you."

"Thank you for not dodging the finality of the last goodbye to BJ. The temptation to avoid it was there: next year somewhere, future medical conventions, or cracked lobster in Crabapple Cove. I was moved witnessing two people acknowledging 'this is it' and, forced by that acknowledgment, saying to each other the important things which need to be said.

I have been with too many people when family members are dying who have not been able to accept 'this is it,' and they forgo the opportunity to remember the special times and share what they have meant to each other. Although it is difficult to express, most of us would not make it without other people who share the burden with us.

Thanks also for not homogenizing the farewells into hugs for everybody. I was glad to see the warm words for some, the tolerable words for Charles, the salutes for Potter, the passionate kiss for Margaret, and the deeply affectionate hug for BJ.

You helped us face the finality of goodbyes and showed us the honesty and courage it takes to express them. I will miss the 4077th."

"I missed the first few years of MASH because it's difficult in a large convent to choose to watch a particular show on the T.V. However, several years ago I 'acquired' my grandmother's little black and white T.V. when she entered a nursing home. Now I never miss an episode and I've managed to see just about all of the old shows as reruns. In fact, the 7 pm MASH reruns (and 11 pm on holidays only) are almost always as sacred to some of us as other Community functions. They are a time to unwind and laugh after a long day in school.

Speaking of school, my Biology students identify 'tracheotomy' as 'what Fr. Mulcahy did,' and 'curare' as 'what Winchester gave to his patient.' In some of our Theology classes the Sisters use MASH for the values it teaches.

Even though MASH has finished production, its reruns will live on, and I look forward to many years of great entertainment."

"The students in Title I reading at South High School in Salt Lake City wish to thank you for all your efforts in making M.A.S.H.

The impact on them has been tremendous. We read the scripts, act out parts, and discuss the series."

"I've watched Mash for about 3 years now. I knew it would have to end sometime and I am kind of glad it is because some shows keep going and repeating everything. You know, it is kind of funny but the letters home to Dad and some of the shows like that have helped me to have a better relationship with my parents and realize I am lucky to have a mom and dad. This may sound weird coming from an 11 year-old girl but it's true. Please keep up the good work and never stop."

```
S-W-A-L-C-A-K-W-S
e i   i a   i o t
a t   c u   s u i
l h   k s   s l c
e       e   d k
d           n
            '
            t
```

"Voici une lettre de ma fille (15 ans a peine)
"Included, a letter from my daughter (just 15)

qui parle et écrit mieux l'anglais que moi. Je ne sais pas comment
who speaks and writes a much better English than me. I don't know how

le dire...mais j'aime MASH...et tout...et tout...
to say it...but I love MASH...and all...and all...

Merci beaucoup, et nous aimons tous MASH."
Thank you very much, we all (like and love) MASH."

"I just saw your
last show (Mash) and a
feeling welled up in
me like I've never
felt before. Now I
know what friendship
means, and how hard I
should hold on to it."

"You showed us so many things;
not only on the war and its misery
but also on life. You always stayed
in this heavy atmosphere with a
smile on the mouth, but we felt the
pressure you had on your shoulders.
You made us realize nobody is
perfect; even army officers couldn't
resist that pressure. You made us
realize everybody makes faults.
     I began to understand myself and
to like myself more. You made me cry
but you made me understand that
crying doesn't arrange anything:
work and effort and perseverance do.
You made me understand staying calm
is important everywhere. You showed
me that there is nothing like home
and nothing like peace. Whenever I'm
depressed, I think of you and I feel
better.
     We'll miss you all a lot. Love
and Peace to you all."

"Tired but enriched, I think I owe you a detailing of how you managed to grab hold of my subconscious last night and rob me of the peaceful sleep I had coveted all day.

You see, along with a few others of my countrymen, last night I viewed 'Goodbye, Farewell and Amen' and, along with a few of the morning-after critics, found it to be good but not great, perhaps necessarily anti-climatic. Or so I thought, I thought. At 11:00, following the last chord of the MASH theme, I proceeded to spend 7 1/2 hours in bed dreaming and/or thinking about what I had seen. In one sequence of my private production I accompanied you and B.J., photographing your last goodbyes. The program had punctured my inner-brain and lodged firmly by its emotional core, compelling and discomforting my mind throughout the night. So thank you for the lost and tossed sleep. You should be very very proud."

"Until about three years ago the word 'mash' brought to my mind potatoes. Now it reminds me of the T.V. program about a M.A.S.H. unit stationed near the front lines in the Korean War. This show has brought me endless hours of laughs, but on the serious side it makes me realize how a war effects the people, and places around them.

Thank you for giving me a view of life I never would have seen without that show."

"My whole family enjoys watching M*A*S*H, sometimes even three times a day. My mom thinks that's a bit much, but my dad says it's the best show on TV. I personally think Hawkeye Pierce is a really funny guy. I like all of the jokes he makes in the O.R.

I want to be a funny actor like you when I grow up. I am ten years old and have a long time to wait. Meanwhile, I keep busy with school and playing with our computer. It doesn't laugh when I tell it jokes though.

I am sorry this is your last year of making M*A*S*H. I hope you can find another job."

"Here in Rockford, Illinois, the leading unemployment city, many of us gave up the 10:00 News to watch MASH, for MASH lets us laugh and forget the sad news we hear all day at work. Radio and TV tells us of more industry closing here and moving out of our city.

MASH distracts us from our depressing area and predicament and gives us renewed hope."

City of Los Angeles

P R O C L A M A T I O N

*WHEREAS, NO TELEVISION SHOW IN HISTORY HAS FACED ITS "FINAL CURTAIN" WITH THE INTEREST, REGRET, POIGNANCY AND FEELING THAT SURROUNDS THE LAST SEASON OF THE TWENTIETH CENTURY-FOX TELEVISION'S "M*A*S*H"; AND*

*WHEREAS, ONE OF THE INDUSTRY'S MOST HONORED SHOWS AS WELL AS ONE OF ITS MOST CONSISTENTLY HIGHEST RATED, "M*A*S*H" BRINGS DOWN THE CURTAIN IN 1982-1983 AFTER ELEVEN YEARS. IN ITS FIRST DECADE THE SERIES GARNERED 99 EMMY NOMINATIONS (WITH FOURTEEN OF THE GOLD STATUETTES); NUMEROUS GOLDEN GLOBES, PEOPLE'S CHOICE, WRITERS GUILD, ACTORS GUILD, HUMANITAS AWARDS AND THE MOST CHERISHED KUDO IN TELEVISION – THE GEORGE FOSTER PEABODY AWARD – THE ONLY COMEDY SO HONORED; AND*

*WHEREAS, IN ADDITION TO ITS NETWORK POPULARITY EVERY MONDAY NIGHT, "M*A*S*H" BECAME THE RUNAWAY SUCCESS STORY OF DOMESTIC SYNDICATION, PLAYING IN SOME MARKETS 16 TIMES A WEEK AND TO 224 MILLION PEOPLE; AND*

WHEREAS, ALAN ALDA, MIKE FARRELL, HARRY MORGAN, LORETTA SWIT, DAVID OGDEN STIERS, JAMIE FARR AND WILLIAM CHRISTOPHER, THE SAME SEVEN STARS OF THE AWARD-WINNING SERIES RELATING TO THE DUTIES OF A MOBILE ARMY SURGERICAL HOSPITAL UNIT DURING THE KOREAN POLICE ACTION, RETURNED FOR THE COMPLETION OF THE ELEVENTH MEMORABLE YEAR. THESE ARE BASICALLY DEDICATED AND SKILLED SURGEONS WHO TURNED TO HUMOR AS RELIEF FROM THE FRONT-LINE HORRORS OF A GRIM MILITARY OPERATION:

*NOW, THEREFORE, I, TOM BRADLEY, MAYOR OF THE CITY OF LOS ANGELES, DO HEREBY PROCLAIM FEBRUARY 28, 1983 AS "M*A*S*H DAY" IN THE CITY OF LOS ANGELES AND COMMEND BURT METCALFE, JOHN RAPPAPORT, THAD MUMFORD, DAN WILCOX, KAREN HALL, STANFORD TISCHLER, OTHER STAFF MEMBERS AND CAST OF "M*A*S*H" FOR THEIR OUTSTANDING ACHIEVEMENTS AND CONTRIBUTIONS TO THE ENTERTAINMENT INDUSTRY, AND EXTEND BEST WISHES FOR CONTINUED SUCCESS IN ALL FUTURE ENDEAVORS.*

FEBRUARY 28, 1983

Tom Bradley
MAYOR

P R O C L A M A T I O N

*WHEREAS, NO TELEVISION SHOW IN HISTORY HAS FACED ITS "FINAL CURTAIN" WITH THE INTEREST, REGRET, POIGNANCY AND FEELING THAT SURROUNDS THE LAST SEASON OF THE TWENTIETH CENTURY-FOX TELEVISION'S "M*A*S*H"; AND*

*WHEREAS, ONE OF THE INDUSTRY'S MOST HONORED SHOWS AS WELL AS ONE OF ITS MOST CONSISTENTLY HIGHEST RATED, "M*A*S*H" BRINGS DOWN THE CURTAIN IN 1982-1983 AFTER ELEVEN YEARS. IN ITS FIRST DECADE THE SERIES GARNERED 99 EMMY NOMINATIONS (WITH FOURTEEN OF THE GOLD STATUETTES); NUMEROUS GOLDEN GLOBES, PEOPLE'S CHOICE, WRITERS GUILD, ACTORS GUILD, HUMANITAS AWARDS AND THE MOST CHERISHED KUDO IN TELEVISION – THE GEORGE FOSTER PEABODY AWARD – THE ONLY COMEDY SO HONORED; AND*

*WHEREAS, IN ADDITION TO ITS NETWORK POPULARITY EVERY MONDAY NIGHT, "M*A*S*H" BECAME THE RUNAWAY SUCCESS STORY OF DOMESTIC SYNDICATION, PLAYING IN SOME MARKETS 16 TIMES A WEEK AND TO 224 MILLION PEOPLE; AND*

WHEREAS, ALAN ALDA, MIKE FARRELL, HARRY MORGAN, LORETTA SWIT, DAVID OGDEN STIERS, JAMIE FARR AND WILLIAM CHRISTOPHER, THE SAME SEVEN STARS OF THE AWARD-WINNING SERIES RELATING TO THE DUTIES OF A MOBILE ARMY SURGERICAL HOSPITAL UNIT DURING THE KOREAN POLICE ACTION, RETURNED FOR THE COMPLETION OF THE ELEVENTH MEMORABLE YEAR. THESE ARE BASICALLY DEDICATED AND SKILLED SURGEONS WHO TURNED TO HUMOR AS RELIEF FROM THE FRONT-LINE HORRORS OF A GRIM MILITARY OPERATION:

*NOW, THEREFORE, I, TOM BRADLEY, MAYOR OF THE CITY OF LOS ANGELES, DO HEREBY PROCLAIM FEBRUARY 28, 1983 AS "M*A*S*H DAY" IN THE CITY OF LOS ANGELES AND COMMEND BURT METCALFE, JOHN RAPPAPORT, THAD MUMFORD, DAN WILCOX, KAREN HALL, STANFORD TISCHLER, OTHER STAFF MEMBERS AND CAST OF "M*A*S*H" FOR THEIR OUTSTANDING ACHIEVEMENTS AND CONTRIBUTIONS TO THE ENTERTAINMENT INDUSTRY, AND EXTEND BEST WISHES FOR CONTINUED SUCCESS IN ALL FUTURE ENDEAVORS.*

FEBRUARY 28, 1983

Postscript

I got a fortuitous assignment from Life magazine. In January 1983, I documented the last shooting week of MASH for them. Ten photos from that exclusive assignment appeared, along with Cindi Stivers' text, in the March 1983 issue. I, however, had taken hundreds of photos in those seven, long, hectic, emotionally-charged days. For this book, I've edited the shoot down to what I believe is a faithful representation of the highlights of that week.

During those last days, I probably spent more time on the set than I had in the entire time the show was on the air. Although Alan Alda is my husband, most of my watching of MASH was done at home in front of the TV set—like the rest of MASH's audience. I loved the show.

In addition to its entertainment value, the show was meticulous in caring about real-life details. Stories were carefully researched and the staff watched over the reality behind the fiction. It was this element of truth that touched me most deeply.

One consistent message came across clearly. War is not only hell, but the legacy of war—destruction of lives, families, traditions, culture, land and property is forever.

In the real wars America has fought in the Far East, we have left children behind—offspring of American servicemen and Asian women—who are scorned, rejected, and unwanted in their homogeneous Asian societies. These children are called Amerasians. They are casualties of war as much as those that have been maimed or buried.

Alan and I are donating our portion of the proceeds of this book to the Pearl S. Buck Foundation, whose work is focused on helping Amerasian children.

Arlene Alda

History of Korea

The Korean people, who for centuries had sought independent development and self-rule in all aspects of their life and culture, found themselves at the turn of this century under the control of Japan, who annexed their country as a Japanese colony in 1910. Korea would remain under Japanese rule for more than four decades.

However, at the Cairo Conference in 1943 the leaders of the United States, Great Britain and China agreed that Korean independence be incorporated in the Cairo declaration. This independence would best be achieved after the defeat of Japan in World War II. This decision was reiterated by the Potsdam Declaration in 1945 and also by the Soviet Union in their declaration of war on Japan, made just eight days before the surrender of the Japanese.

But immediate Korean independence was circumvented by an agreement between the United States, Great Britain and the Soviet Union at the Yalta Conference in February of 1945. This agreement called for an international trusteeship for Korea but it did not specify an exact plan for governing Korea. However, it was decided that Korea would be divided for the express purpose of effectively disarming the Japanese military. The Soviet Union would occupy the northern portion of Korea above the 38th Parallel, while the United States occupied the southern portion of the peninsula below the 38th Parallel. The 38th Parallel was chosen solely to promote quick and effective military operations on behalf of the Allied forces.

The Soviet Union stationed their troops in North Korea and almost immediately enacted their own military government, which would in time establish the North Korean Communist regime.

Consequently, the Allied foreign ministers convened in Moscow late in 1945 and decided to impose a trusteeship over Korea that would extend for a five-year period, during which time Korea would prepare for complete independence. This proposal was rejected by the Korean people, who desired a unified and independent country. This desire was never realized.

Furthermore, the following year a joint commission of the United States and the Soviet Union met in Seoul for the express purpose of establishing a unified government for this divided nation. The joint commission was unable to reach an agreement on a unified Korea.

Other attempts throughout 1947 failed to resolve the question of Korean independence and the United States, now frustrated with the Soviet Union's uncooperative position, turned to the United Nations for assistance. A United Nations resolution in that same year recognized Korea's right to form their own government, made provisions for the withdrawal of occupational forces and called for elections throughout Korea, under the supervision of a U.N. commission.

But the Soviets would not permit entry of the U.N. commission into the Soviet-held North Korean territory. So in 1948 elections were held only in the southern half of the country, below the 38th Parallel. A national assembly was elected, a Constitution was adopted and the Republic of Korea came into existence.

Less than one month later, North Korea established the Democratic People's Republic of Korea, a communist regime which claimed authority over both North and South Korea.

By mid 1949, the United States had withdrawn its occupational forces, leaving only a staff of military advisors in South Korea. The Republic of Korea and the United States developed a provisional military pact and established economic aid through the Economic Cooperation Administration.

The Soviet Union also removed its occupational forces from North Korea and signed several agreements with the Democratic People's Republic of Korea, providing military and economic aid. This North Korean government then established relations with China, which would prove most helpful in the very near future.

As far back as 1946, the North Korean communists were reorganizing and reinforcing their armed forces. Many North Korean youths were taken to the Soviet Union for military training. By 1950, the communist North Korean forces had swollen to nearly 200,000 men. Soviet military equipment including tanks and planes were sent to North Korea. The ultimate objective of the North Korean Government was to overtake South Korea through military invasion.

—William J. McGuire

Korean War

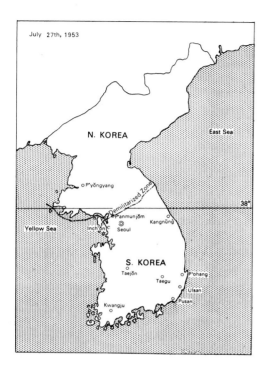

KOREA

On June 25, 1950, North Korean military forces crossed the 38th Parallel, attacked and quickly overran the South Korean Army. Seoul, the capital of South Korea, fell to the enemy by the third day of the invasion. By August, the South Korean Army had been systematically pushed and cornered into the southeast end of their country, leaving the entire peninsula in the hands of the North Korean forces.

The Republic of South Korea appealed to the United Nations for assistance. The U.N. passed a resolution ordering the North Koreans to withdraw to the 38th Parallel. Also, all member-nations of the U.N. were asked to give military support to the Republic of South Korea. The United States responded by ordering the use of U.S. troops, planes and ships against the North Koreans.

In September of that same year, General Douglas MacArthur, commanding-general of the U.N. forces, directed an amphibious assault at Inchon on the western coast of South Korea. The initial and quick successes of the North Korean Army were altered, and the course of the war suddenly changed.

In the following weeks of fierce fighting, the North Korean troops were expelled from South Korean territory. The U.N. and South Korean forces then pushed far into North Korea and it seemed as though the war would soon end with the defeat of North Korea.

But in October, the communist Chinese came to the aid of the North Korean Army. The U.N. and South Korean advancements into North Korea were quickly checked. The communist Chinese, entering the war in massive numbers, forced a major retreat of U.N. forces into South Korea. Seoul once again fell into enemy hands.

The U.N. and South Korean forces regrouped and soon counter-attacked, driving the communists from Seoul in mid-March. The front lines of both sides were drawn roughly along the 38th Parallel, the very line that separated the two nations before the fighting began.

Virtually, the entire peninsula was subject to the ruins of war and many major cities were almost totally destroyed. The U.N. forces, comprised of fifteen member-nations, contributed men and supplies to the support of South Korea. The Soviet Union aided the North Koreans and the communist Chinese with military supplies, fuel, food and medicine. Casualties on both sides were severe. The U.N. forces reported 71,500 killed, 250,000 wounded and 83,263 missing in action. The South Korean casualties were 400,000 wounded/killed. The communist wounded/killed in the war totaled 1,349,000, bringing the total killed or wounded to 2,151,763.

The Korean War ended with the signing of a peace treaty at P'anmunjom, North Korea some 37 months and 2 days after the North Korean invasion of South Korea. Yet, even as the 18 copies of the main truce; six in English, six in Korean, and six in Chinese, were being signed, the sound of artillery guns could still be heard, as both sides continued the struggle until the final hour of truce, 10:00 P.M., July 27, 1953.

—W. J. M.

Pearl S. Buck Foundation

Amerasians are half-American and half-Asian children, born of American servicemen and other U.S. Nationals from liaisons with Asian women. The term, Amerasian, was coined by the late Nobel and Pulitzer Prize-winning author, Pearl S. Buck, to describe these mixed-race, mixed-national and cross-cultural offspring and to fix co-equal responsibility for these needy ones.

In Asia, the father is key to the record of birth, to citizenship, to education and to initial employment. If the father is absent, not only are these avenues closed to the child, but without proper record of birth, the children legally do not exist!

While America views itself as a "melting pot," Asian nations view themselves as "pure" and negatively view mixed-race as an adulteration, and worse. As a result, the Amerasian can only hold "second class citizenship," if he or she is not declared "stateless." Thus they suffer daily from the unofficial yet all pervading blind prejudice that makes them among the poorest of the poor in every Asian country.

The Pearl S. Buck Foundation, with the aid of concerned Americans, is working to provide a hopeful future for Amerasian children in Korea, Okinawa, the Philippines, Taiwan, and Thailand. The foundation is constantly seeking the right to offer program services to Amerasians within the Socialist Republic of Vietnam. Presently, more than 5,000 Amerasian children are enrolled in Pearl S. Buck Foundation sponsorship programs, while nearly 7,000 other Amerasians receive various indirect non-sponsorship services.

Specifically the Foundation's purposes are (1) to educate the American public to the existence and needs of the Amerasian children and the American responsibility to them; (2) to educate the Amerasian children so that they will, when adults, be responsible, productive human beings—a credit to both sides of their ancestry; (3) to build a climate of social acceptance for these children in the countries of their birth.

The Pearl S. Buck Foundation has offered sustenance to the Amerasians while bringing the issue to the American public via public service announcements on radio and TV, and in the glossy magazines. Cooperation with the media has produced notable articles in prestigious publications such as the *New York Times Magazine,* the *L.A. Times,* and the *Washington Post.* Articles have appeared in *Parade,* the *Christian Science Monitor,* and *Reader's Digest.* The Foundation served as technical advisor to the popular CBS TV series, M*A*S*H, in the episode, "Yessir, That's Our Baby!". The episode was shown to the American public on two occasions and reached an estimated audience of 45 million viewers.

Perhaps the purpose of the Foundation can best be summarized in Pearl S. Buck's own words. "First, let me say that this is the only agency to which I have ever given, or will ever give, my own name. I have done so because after twenty-five years of experience in the field of lost and needy children, I have come to believe that the most effective efforts on their behalf are usually initiated by individuals who have a deep concern for human justice. . . The purpose of the Foundation is to publicize and eliminate injustice and prejudice suffered by children who, because of their birth, are not permitted to enjoy the social, economic and civil privileges normally accorded to children. . ."

Pearl Sydenstricker Buck was born June 26, 1892 in Hillsboro, West Virginia. When she was five months old her parents, who were missionaries, took her to China with them. She spent approximately thirty years of her life there. Her first story-telling influences stemmed from three primary sources, her Chinese nurse, her father's adventures in China and her mother's childhood years in West Virginia.

Pearl S. Buck won many awards, including both the Pulitzer Prize and Nobel Prize for Literature, numerous citations, and more than a dozen honorary degrees from various colleges and universities.

Ms. Buck died in 1973 shortly before her eighty-first birthday. The United States government honored her in June of 1983 by issuing the Pearl S. Buck postage stamp.

The Pearl S. Buck Foundation is headquartered at her home, Green Hills Farm, Bucks County, Pennsylvania.

—W. J. M.

Arlene Alda has been a photographer since 1968. Her work has appeared in *Pageant, New York, Redbook, Ladies Home Journal, Vogue, Today's Health, MS., People, US,* and *Life* magazines. She has had exhibits in New York's Nikon House, Soho Gallery, and Modernage Gallery.

Ms. Alda's photographs have been included in several books, including *Broadway Musicals, Women Photograph Men,* and *Women of Vision.*

She is the photographer/author of *On Set, Arlene Alda's ABC, Sonya's Mommy Works* and *Matthew and His Dad* (October 1983 - Simon and Schuster).

Ms. Alda is half of the team of Alda and Alda who are proud of their creative efforts as manifest in their three daughters, Eve, Elizabeth and Beatrice.

Alan Alda played Hawkeye Pierce in the MASH television series for eleven years. During that time he wrote 23 half-hour segments and directed 36.

He was nominated for 25 Emmys and won Emmys in all three categories as writer, actor and director.

Along with ''Same Time, Next Year'' and ''California Suite,'' his recent films include ''The Seduction of Joe Tynan,'' which he wrote and played in, and ''The Four Seasons'' which he wrote, directed and acted in.

The other half of Alda and Alda is also very proud of their daughters.

Publisher's Acknowledgements

CREDITS

PRODUCTION COORDINATION AND DESIGN
Sharon Brady

INTERNATIONAL PRINTING LIAISON
DNP (America), New York, New York

PRINTING & BINDING
Dai Nippon Printing Company, Ltd., Tokyo, Japan

COLOR SEPARATIONS
Dai Nippon Printing Company, Ltd., Tokyo, Japan

TYPOGRAPHY
John Scott Typesetting Company, Jersey City, New Jersey

SPECIAL TYPOGRAPHY AND REPRODUCTION PHOTOGRAPHY
TGIF, Fairfield, New Jersey

REPRODUCTION PHOTOGRAPHY
Comphoto, Mountain Lakes, New Jersey

SPECIAL REPRODUCTION PHOTOGRAPHY
The Color Wheel, New York, New York

ADDITIONAL REPRODUCTION PHOTOGRAPHY
The Print Factory, Verona, New Jersey

SPECIAL GRAPHICS
Spectrum Press, Orange, New Jersey

KOREAN TEXT
William J. McGuire

SPECIAL THANKS
Arlene Alda
Alan Alda
Martin Bregman
Yoh Jinno
Rosemary Chiaverini
Greg Hildebrandt
Gerri Slater

ADDITIONAL THANKS

John Brady
Sally Brady
Pat Diehl
Pete Dominick
Dena Hansen
Marta Friedland
Betty McGuire
Sachihiko Oribe
Stephen Pokotilow
Sharon Power

Cynthia Rauschberg
Mike Rauschberg
Joe Riley
John Scott
Kathleen Scott
Matt Scott
Joseph Scrocco, Sr.
Jeannie Scrocco
Jim Sirmans
Karen White

The Pearl S. Buck Foundation

Staff and Crew of the Final Season of Mash

EXECUTIVE PRODUCER	Burt Metcalfe		PROPERTY MASTER	Doug Stubbs
SUPERVISING PRODUCER	John Rappaport		ASSISTANT PROPERTY MASTER	J.W. Biggs
PRODUCER	Thad Mumford		MEN'S COSTUMER	Albert Frankel
PRODUCER	Dan Wilcox		MEN'S COSTUMER	Barry Kellogg
ASSOCIATE PRODUCER	Stan Tischler		WOMEN'S COSTUMER	Rita Bennett
EXECUTIVE SCRIPT CONSULTANT	Karen Hall		MAKEUP ARTIST	Terry Miles
EXECUTIVE PRODUCTION MANAGER	Mark Evans		HAIR STYLIST	Carol Pershing
PRODUCTION SUPERVISOR	Dick Glassman		CRAFT SERVICEMAN	Rick Chavez
UNIT PRODUCTION MANAGER	David Hawks		TECHNICAL ADVISOR	Rita Hudis
1ST ASSISTANT DIRECTOR	Cathy Kinsock		UNIT PUBLICITY	Chuck Panama
2ND ASSISTANT DIRECTOR	Barbara Gelman		MECHANICAL EFFECTS	Jay King
SCRIPT SUPERVISOR	Roberta Scelza		DIALOGUE COACH	Marty Lowenheim
DIRECTOR OF PHOTOGRAPHY	Dominick R. Palmer, Jr.		CASTING	Joyce Robinson
CAMERA OPERATOR	Bob Casey		CASTING	Penny Ellers
1ST ASSISTANT CAMERAMAN	Travers Hill, Jr.		CASTING	Joan Papazian
2ND ASSISTANT CAMERAWOMAN	Patricia Hill		PRODUCTION COORDINATOR	Robert Metoyer
ART DIRECTOR	John Leimanis		SECRETARY TO EXEC. PRODUCER	Dona Nicoloff
SET DECORATOR	Bert Allen		SECRETARY TO SUPV. PRODUCER	Melissa Towler
LEAD MAN	Bob Steffensen		SECRETARY TO PRODUCERS	Miriam Brody
CONSTRUCTION COORDINATOR	Ron Moser		PRODUCTION SECRETARY	Lynne Davies-Baca
GAFFER	Larry Rake		SHOW AUDITOR	Rita Raffo
BEST BOY	Chuck Bateman		TRANSPORTATION COORDINATOR	John Hood
KEY GRIP	Jim Robinson		POSTPRODUCTION SUPERVISOR	Joseph Silver
2ND GRIP	Michael Kenner		EDITOR	Stan Tischler
CRAB DOLLY OPERATOR	Chuck Lantz		ASSISTANT EDITOR	Ron Smith
SOUND MIXER	Will Yarbrough		EDITOR	Larry Mills
SOUND BOOM MAN	Phil Mitchell, Jr.		ASSISTANT EDITOR	Willie Navarro
SOUND UTILITY TECHNICIAN	Patricia Barbeau		RANCH RANGER	Kent Hartwell